Journey With Me

to

Personal & Professional Success

A Discussion of Personal and Professional Core Practices

BY TINA MITCHELL

Published by Publish Promptly
10061 Talbert Avenue, Suite 218
Fountain Valley, California 92708 USA
PublishPromptly.com

DEDICATION

To My Mom - Beth Samuelson

Mom, how did you find the strength to be the mom you were with all of our life challenges? How were you inspirational when everything around you was so difficult? How were you always there for me when no one was around for you? How did you love me unconditionally during times when I didn't show my appreciation? I see now, that it was the love for Karen and me that kept you going, and I thank you Mom for all that you gave me!

To My Dad - Gerald Frisbey

Your life was difficult but you kept your burden well hidden and were always there for me, protecting me from dark realities because I was daddy's little girl. You're no longer with us, but I know you knew how much I loved you. For my spunky personality, my stubbornness and my ability to have fun in everything I do, I give credit to you. Thank you Dad. I love you and RIP!

To My Baby Sister - Karen Kelley

We are so much alike and at the same time so different. I am extremely proud of the woman you have become. The wife you are, the mother you are, and the faith you have. I am proud to say I am your big sister. I love you, little sis!

To My Husband - Dave Mitchell

You have always been there for me, sacrificing your happiness at times to ensure mine. Supportive, loyal and loving in your own special way. My life would not be what it is today without you as a part of it. I love you today more than yesterday. I will love you more tomorrow than today. How beautiful our love is that it continues to grow every day. I can't wait to see how strong our love will be for every tomorrow to come.

To My Daughter - Stephanie Mitchell

You are not my biological daughter, but I consider you my daughter in every other way. You have been such a special part of my life. I thank you for allowing me to step in and be your mom #2. Embracing me the way you did from the first day we met, and continuing to embrace me in your adult life. You have made me feel as though I am special in your life. My love for you is as my mom's love is for me. I love you, sweetheart!

To My Friend - April Mirabella

Thank you for sharing your first daughter and your first born with me. I know the special bond the two of you have. As an outsider being welcomed in to share the gift of motherhood, words alone cannot show my appreciation and the love I have for you. We have many years ahead as we continue to experience special moments in our daughter's life. I love you!

TABLE OF CONTENTS

FOREWORD

By Hal Elrod

Tina Mitchell has done something that less than one-tenth of one percent of human beings will ever do - openly share her journey of overcoming challenges and achieving extraordinary success, and put it into a book that can help YOU overcome your own challenges and take your personal and professional success to new heights.

In Journey With Me, Tina shares tools and resources to take your life and business to a high level. Consider that wherever you are in your life right now is both temporary, and exactly where you are supposed to be (otherwise you would be somewhere else). You are always exactly where you need to be, experiencing what you need to experience, so that you can learn what you must learn; in order to become the person you need to be, to create everything you want for your life. Always.

Any time you find yourself "wishing" you were further along than you are, or comparing where you are with where someone else is, keep in mind that when you finally get to the point you've been working towards for so long, you never wish it would have happened any sooner. Instead, you see that your journey and the timing are perfect.

So, be at peace with where you are while maintaining a healthy sense of urgency, to make the consistent progress each day that will ensure you get to wherever it is that you want to go. Tina Mitchell is your mentor and Journey With Me is your guide. Like any great mentor, Tina and her book will get you where you want to go, much faster than you would be able to get there on your own.

Congratulations on picking up Tina's book. I can't wait to see the impact it's going to make in your life.

With gratitude,

Hal Elrod, author of the #1 bestselling book, The Miracle Morning: The Not-So-Obvious Secret Guaranteed to Transform Your Life... (Before 8AM)

INTRODUCTION

My book is based on my six personal and professional core practices. In my book I will share in great detail each of my core practices while weaving in my personal life experiences from the age of 7 until today.

I have had many successes during my life journey. However, only after reading about my failures can you fully understand how I got to my core practices. My journey has been exciting and also at times pretty traumatic, but without these life lessons I would not be the person I am today and would not be able to share with you the knowledge I have gained from them.

I will share how at a young age I succeeded in selling Girl Scout cookies and being featured in the newspaper every year. You'll read the story of how I went from picking strawberries in the fields to becoming the Strawberry Picking Champion. You'll also discover that as a young violinist I was chosen to travel to Aberdeen Scotland for a world festival. I will share how in my adult life I was named in the top 1% of mortgage professionals in the nation, developed mortgage software and started a software company. I will also share the effect my dad's attempted suicide had on my life and how as a young child I played my violin at Pike Place Market with my sister to help keep a roof over our heads. I will share other trying events, from how my first husband was incarcerated for many years to the tragic loss of my daughter Amber. You'll see how the financial meltdown profoundly affected my personal and professional life.

When writing this book I made the decision to get up close and personal. I decided to be vulnerable and not leave any of my important stories out. These stories shaped my life and the person I am today. I hope by reading the good and bad in my life you will be able to embrace your successes as well as your failures, as I have.

I'm excited to take you on this journey with me; a journey to "live your dream now!"

My Personal Core Practices

▸ Dream

"Happiness is simple. Have a dream, the intention to make it happen and a plan to get there."

- Tina Mitchell

Every day I dream. I come by it naturally. As a young girl, my mother would take my sister and me to the Tacoma, Washington train station when times were tough. Together we spent hours imagining the lives of the travelers as we people watched. Many mindful hours helped me to see who I was and who I wanted to be. Many focused hours taught me to understand the power of a dream.

As you travel through this book, I hope that you, like me, catch a glimpse of how dreaming can change your life path and guide your personal and professional journey. My goal is to help you see clearly how you can live your dream and visualize your way to a new reality.

*** My Motto: Live Your Dream Now ***

▸ *Be Alert*

"Wake every morning alert to all the surprises waiting just for you. They show up everywhere when you're watching for them and what an amazing day it will be!"

- Tina Mitchell

To be alert is to not miss a moment in your life. It's about creating "positive triggers" you can go to when something is not going your way or you feel someone is treating you unfairly. The small things will bring you the happiness you are looking for in your life.

If you watch for the small miracles, they show up every day, all day. If you are waiting for the big ones, you may be waiting a long time. Why not focus on all the good and beauty in life? Your day will always have something to smile about if you are alert to the small things.

▸ *Learn to Fail*

"Life is balanced with no exceptions. Every failure has a gain waiting on the other side. Make the decision to look for the gain and not focus on the loss."

- Tina Mitchell

Life is not just about succeeding, it's also about rejoicing in your failures. Only after accepting that failures are part of the process, was I able to benefit from them. You may ask, "How?" The lessons you will learn and the knowledge you will gain from those failures will prepare you as you move forward in your life.

Failures are part of life and no one can escape them. So why not embrace them?

My Professional Core Practices

▸ *"One-Time" Your Business*

"Take control of your business or your business will control you."

- Tina Mitchell

Have you ever left the office after a long day wondering what you've accomplished only to wake up the next morning anxious and overwhelmed? Anticipation of what the day ahead holds because of the tasks left undone from the day before will create those feelings.

We all have been there. Let me help you by sharing my "one-time your business" philosophy.

▸ *Embrace Your Strengths*

"Embrace your strengths and live a successful personal and professional life."

- Tina Mitchell

Have you ever said to yourself "I can do everything myself" and then realized you cannot? You have strengths and weaknesses; you love to do some things and hate to do others. It's time to hire a team and enjoy your life.

Embracing your strengths is all about building a team.

▸ *Get Connected*

"Connect with people on a deeper level and they will want to support your life and business."

- Tina Mitchell

Are you having a hard time connecting to the people you want to know? No matter how talented or smart you are, if you don't connect with others, it will be difficult to get the job you want; build great working relationships with your colleagues; gain and retain clients; and attract the people you need to support your business.

As you learn to embrace my personal and professional core practices, I know you will find your challenges easier and your successes more frequent.

I will share tools and resources to take your life and business to the highest level.

By engaging in my 6 core practices explained in this book, you will see that you have EVERYTHING you need in life. I will provide you the tools needed to get EVERYTHING you want in life!

I believe each of our lives is like a road trip. When traveling, you use a map to get from one destination to another. Even with a map you can take wrong turns, but you are able to adjust and take a different road if you choose. There are signs along the way with life lessons and, the road you take will determine your life direction and life experiences.

Your life is a journey, a journey of discovery, a discovery of who you are and what you have to contribute to this world.

I'm excited to take you on this journey with me. Thank you in advance for taking time out of your life to be a part of my experience. I know you will not feel it was time wasted.

- Tina Mitchell

CHAPTER 1 - DREAM

"Happiness is simple. Have a **dream**, the intention to make it happen and a plan to get there."

- Tina Mitchell

As a child, I wasn't sure who I was or what I would contribute to this world, but life soon taught me the value of dreams. At a very young age I realized that dreaming and visualization were essential parts of reaching any goal, and they became my "tools" for success. I learned to dream big.

Do you take time to dream?

It really doesn't matter what you are dreaming about as long as you dream BIG!

Family... Community... Spirituality... Success... Career... All are dream worthy!

When you dream, you allow your subconscious to engage on the topic and work on your dream. You release your mind to imagine, so you are operating from imagination, not memory. Imagination includes the ability to visualize and can create intense and expansive dreams.

In my younger years I was not as intentional with visualization as I am now, as an adult, because I didn't realize what I was doing and the power of a dream. It was just a part of me. I didn't use any of the techniques that I use now and will share with you later. The only thing I did was imagine it.

As a child I thought my dad was the greatest father in the world. As daddy's little girl I felt special and the bond we had could not be broken. My little sister was always doing things with my mom and my strongest bond was with my dad.

I can see and hear it as if it was yesterday, my dad and I dancing to Abba and screaming as loud as we could along with the lyrics, "You are the dancing queen, young and sweet, only seventeen, dancing queen, feel the beat from the tambourine." These were moments back in time that I will never forget. They were special moments between just my dad and me.

The memories I have of my dad will never fade. The magic tricks he did, playing with me for hours, laughing all the time and just living life! The problem was he didn't know how to deal with life. He was an alcoholic and addicted to amphetamines. He was not mean when he was drunk or drugged, but instead it made him crazy fun. The reality was he was not happy and was masking his depression. He could not hold down a job, and made it very stressful for my mom.

My mom wanted to shelter my little sister and me to protect us from the reality during our childhood. She always figured out the details and somehow pulled everything together and made sure we had a roof over our heads.

My mom was a train fanatic. I remember many trips to the Tacoma, Washington train station at one or two o'clock in the morning. My mom would wake us up and say, "Girls we're going to the train station. Get your favorite stuffed animal and blanket." We would go to the train station and sit outside, sometimes staying there for hours, from late at night until early in the morning.

Tina Mitchell

My mom would tell us stories of where we were going. We knew we were not going anywhere, but those long hours are where visualization evolved for me. When we would occasionally stop by during the day, and I would watch families board the train in their fancy clothes and imagine where they were going. I would try to figure out how they became who they were. I would imagine myself in their shoes, so to speak. At night I held on to the memories of those people but would see myself, instead of them.

We went to the train station often, and it was our usual routine, because it was my mom's way to release her stress. Once older, my sister and I realized that she also took us there for our safety. She didn't want us around my dad when he got too drunk. It wasn't until I was 9 or 10 years old that I realized the problems my dad really had. He wasn't abusive or mad, just fun, but my mom didn't feel it was a safe environment for her girls.

As an adult I now realize that the train station was the time and the place where I learned how to visualize. Visualization has hugely impacted my life. What a blessing these long hours of visualizing were for me.

We thought of the train station as mom's special place. To this day, my mom lives in a little house in a small town in Elbe, Washington, just 12 miles from Mount Rainier. The Mount Rainier Scenic Railroad tourist train goes right past her backyard every day. In this little town there's a motel where each room is its own separate caboose. Located in that same town is the Mount Rainier Dining Company restaurant, which is an actual railroad dining car.

What a perfect place for my mom to live! She has lived there for many years with my stepdad! My mom is now retired and able to volunteer for Trails & Rails. It's run by the National Park Service. Her involvement allows her to travel on the train, while volunteering her time as a guide sharing the history of all the places where the train travels. She gets eight trips a season which will total over 250 hours a year traveling on the train and living her dream. Growing up my mom's dream was for her girls to have a better life. Now that we are adults, she can have dreams for herself.

When you visualize, it's critically important to be done in the moment!

What and how do you visualize?

Having trouble understanding visualization? Listed below are some techniques I often share with people looking to create a safe space to dream.

▸ **Sit in a quiet room with music and visualize your dream.**
A quiet place is key to get into the space to dream and to really draw out your imagination. A quiet place allows you to get deep into the moment.

▸ **Make a vision poster board.**
A poster board is a great tool that you can pin up on your wall in your office or home. The experience when making it is also an important part of the process. I suggest that you update and change it up to keep it new, which will allow you to experience the process repeatedly. Using a board made of cloth and Velcro® tape makes it easy to change.

▸ **Build a vision board movie using technology.**
There are free online resources. The one I have used is Stupeflix and it's very user friendly. Many other resources are available for creating video board movies and online vision boards. I love the web based

application vision boards because your images move and you can add music to enhance your viewing experience.

- **Write down your life as if it's a story book that you can read often.**

The experience of writing your story can be very powerful. Seeing your story (or the story you want to create) in print makes it more real. You will find as you do this, that soon you are reading a book about the life that you are already living. This is the purpose of visualization.

- **Scribble your dream life out on a notepad, as if you were drawing a cartoon and are the character in your own life movie.**

This is the same as writing a story, but instead with pictures. You can do this in book format or on a poster board.

- **Have an imaginary friend and talk about your dream with them, just as you may have done as a child.**

As a child I did this all the time. I didn't know why I was doing it, but it was fun. When practicing my violin, I imagined people were watching me. I also talked to myself vocally about my dream life and pretended someone was listening.

- **Stare at the sky and visualize.**

I think we can all agree that clouds and the sky are magical. I love to lie on the grass, stare at the clouds and visualize my entire future life. It's positively spectacular how you can get lost in the clouds with your thoughts, imagining the most spectacular things. Anything is possible!

At night I love to look at the stars as if each one was waiting to manifest anything I want for my future.

I love nature and exploring it anytime I have time for myself. If I'm outside camping in the woods, at the beach, on the lake or river, I am always visualizing the life that I have designed for myself. I take any and every opportunity to visualize and dream.

Having all or a combination of these will make your visualization fun and prevent any boredom. Rotate through them to keep it new and exciting. You don't want to get bored and not continue because all of these tools can help you to visualize, and visualization is powerful!

Visualization is an important part of making your dreams come true, and should be part of your daily routine.

See the person you want to become.

You can just live life or design the life you want to live!

Get busy living your life or your life will live you!

Give yourself the gift of time. Take time for yourself to visualize and watch how your life will change.

I will share later the best time of day to regularly visualize. You want to visualize any moment you have but just like other regular routines you want to have visualization as one of them. Routines are things you do every day, at the approximate same time of the day.

Another important part of reaching your dream, is to share it with others. You have to talk about your dream with others, especially people you care about. Those around you may say you can't do it, but don't let that get to you. It makes me sad when I hear people say these people don't want you to succeed. I don't believe this is true. The people who are close to you may do this because they are most attached to the outcome, and the idea of you shooting for the stars may scare them. A spouse may be afraid of the loss of income if you give up security to reach for your dream. A parent may be afraid of you failing and the hurt you may experience. They're just trying to protect you. These are valid concerns for them because it's not their dream. It's your dream, you know you can do it and you will, if you believe in yourself. It won't become real if you keep it a secret. If you believe in your dream, fight for it and don't give up, your naysayers will eventually join the ride.

When someone tells you "you can't," this can be your biggest motivator if you embrace it! Show them you can!

I have realized for myself that preparation is also a powerful part of visualization. While using these techniques and going through the preparation, you want to embrace that moment and remember the feelings you had through the process. This too will help to manifest your dreams.

To be successful all you need is...
Belief, Confidence, and Hard Work.

It's not hard to be successful. The hard part is believing you can.

If you believe in yourself that will build the confidence you need to succeed. If your dream is big enough you will work really hard and do anything to get it!

Believe in yourself more than anyone else ever could. Learn to dream, and the visualization techniques will enhance your chances because you are more intentional. However, even with ALL the visualization techniques, you will not be successful if you don't believe in yourself, have confidence and a willingness to work hard.

My first memory of turning a dream into reality reaches back to when I was 7 years old. In fact, I used visualization as a tool when I was a Girl Scout! I sold girl scout cookies and even at this young age I wanted to win the honor of the most cookie sales. I wanted to go to camp and to do so, I needed to sell a lot of Girl Scout cookies because my parents could not afford to send me. Other kids had their parents sell their cookies for them at their work. My mom was a stay at home mom and my dad, when he was working, didn't have the opportunity, like my fellow troop members' parents did.

I knew that if I wanted to realize my dream of riding horses at camp, I was going to have to work hard for it. As I was going door to door to sell my cookies, I would envision the homeowner answering and not just buying one box of cookies, but purchasing many. When the homeowner answered the door, I would smile as big as I could and entice them to want to purchase with my best script.

"My name is Tina Frisbey and I have some amazing cookies for sale. My favorites are the mint chocolate cookies, but I have many more to choose from. Which one is your favorite that you would like to purchase?" If they said, "No, thank you," I would always have a follow up script. "You would be purchasing for a very good cause. I love Girl Scout camp and really want to go. The only way I will be able to get there is if I sell enough cookies. Can you help me get to camp?" I had a high selling ratio because I didn't let "no thank you" stop me. Usually they would buy more than one box after hearing my reason and seeing my determination.

Enjoy what you do, and people will want to help you. Act as if you don't want to be there and they will sense this and be more likely not to support you. Your actions and feelings are contagious!

I would also sit outside the Safeway store every Saturday and Sunday to sell my cookies. I watched shoppers walk past me into the store with their heads down as if they were trying to ignore me and pretend I wasn't even there. I would visualize them coming out and buying. I would even visualize a line of people waiting to purchase from me, and you know what? It worked! It didn't just work because I visualized it, but because I was able to smile as they passed me going into the store and again, as they came out.

How could they not stop after seeing my smile and the confidence I had? If they did pass by, I would follow and gently say, "Excuse me, I have amazing cookies that are only available during the Girl Scout season and I wouldn't want you to miss out." While I chased them down, my mom stayed behind and continue collecting money from those waiting to purchase. It's funny to think that even at such a young age, I prepared my script to close the deal.

I was motivated, and if I wanted to go to camp I had to do it on my own. I have to admit I needed my mom's help because I was too young to go door to door on my own, but I had to beg my mom to let me stay out later and keep knocking. By 8 or 9 p.m. she insisted we wrap it up for the night. She would say, "There's always tomorrow, honey." I had a little late start when going door to door because my mom would insist I get my violin practicing in before I started selling my cookies. It also was not my mom's favorite thing to do on a weekend. I'm sure she didn't appreciate standing out in the cold and sometimes rain at Safeway, but she did. THANK YOU MOM!

I became the top Girl Scout sales girl in Federal Way, Washington, selling the most cookies every year. I was the youngest to achieve that! My first year I remember selling 400 boxes, with my closest competitor only selling 200! I was only 7 years old! Seeing myself in the Federal Way paper every year and embracing that moment as the photographer took my picture, made me realize my dreams could come true! It was addictive.

In subsequent years, I maintained my cookie sales success and helped my sister Karen sell as well, so both of us could go to camp. My dream was shared and became our vision. Karen didn't really want to sell the cookies but did it because her big sister did. Together we sold enough boxes for both of us to attend camp, and she appeared in the Federal Way paper too. Watching those dreams become reality was very powerful for me.

During these same years I was dreaming about being a professional concert violinist. Not all dreams will come true, this dream of mine did not because I let life take me down. I will talk in more detail about this in the discussion of my personal core practice, *Learn To Fail.*

As a child I studied the violin, from the time I was four years old. I practiced for 2 to 3 hours a day. There were many times that my mom would dress my sister and me up in matching bicentennial outfits and bonnets and take us downtown to Pike Place Market. We played as street performers to help earn money to keep a roof over our heads.

We were the Frisbey (my maiden name) girls. As I got older I became embarrassed and afraid my friends would walk by and see me. I remember pulling my bonnet over my forehead in hopes of not being recognized. Still I was a Frisbey girl, so I played my violin and pictured myself in a different place. This was a time when I would imagine and visualize being anywhere but where I was.

We didn't have much money, but somehow my mom found a way to get us violin lessons. No small feat, but my mom was persistent! We studied with amazing teachers over the years, including Dr. Martin Friedman, a music instructor at the Cornish College of the Arts. For many years Dr. Friedman bought our violins for us and taught us for a small fraction of his going rate. I don't know how many times my mom knocked on his door before he finally said yes, but I do know that she would not give up.

She fought for her girls. She realized that our family dynamic could mean fewer opportunities and she sought to change that. She wanted to give my sister and me the gift of music and she wanted us to study with the best!

My mom focused on a solution and continually found ways to help my sister and me excel as musicians. We played everywhere, from the Pike Place Market street corner to the women's lounge on the train, and gained self-confidence and skill. My mom gave us more than the gift of music and self-worth. She gave us the drive to see past immediate problems, envision our realities and create success.

Reaching new levels of expertise on my violin was my dream for many years. I loved to compete against other kids who worked hard and had unbelievable talent, and I unknowingly used visualization to push myself to higher levels of performance.

I really mastered my visualization techniques with the violin. My dream was big even as a young violinist. I dreamed about becoming a professional concert violinist, playing all over the world. I remember I would visualize competing and I could actually see the judges smiling, awed by my performance. In my dream I won every time! I could see myself getting the trophy. I would look at the trophies I already had in my room and imagine the next one lined up on the shelf. I could actually see the trophy being presented to me on stage and would embrace the feeling I would have accepting my award.

Part of my dream of being a professional concert violinist and playing my violin around the world came true. I traveled to at least one continent out of the US, Europe. I went to Aberdeen, Scotland to be part of the International Festival of Youth Orchestras.

The opportunity manifested itself at the age of 12, the summer before junior high. Several members of the Thalia Symphony, where I played the violin were chosen. The finest players were to travel to Europe and I wanted to go. I could "see" it and "feel" it, and it was my dream. As I competed, I recalled my visualization. I could see myself playing flawlessly. I was awarded a scholarship to pay for the trip. Once there, I competed with kids from all over the world to be one of the selected few to play in the Festival Orchestra. We all came together and played in one symphony; many of my fellow members did not even speak English, including our conductor. I can't even write how this experience felt. What I can say is my love of music today was largely due to the experience of being part of something so wonderful and so phenomenal! I would later reflect back to this moment often.

Because I felt the magic of visualization as a young child, I lived many of my dreams during my younger years. The clearer you are about your life, the more powerful your life will be.

I am a believer in the power of dreams!

I know that dreams can come true. I've seen it in my own life... personally and professionally, time after time. Dreaming is central to my success and has shaped who I am today. Dreams allow me to explore, to test my boundaries and to triumph.

Are you going to live the life you were given or live the life you dream of?

Make your dream so clear that you wake up and walk right into it!

What is your dream, a dream so big you can taste it, feel it and see yourself in that dream; a dream worth fighting for?

If you can dream it, you can do it!

When you chase your dreams, it builds courage. Courage will help you achieve amazing success in life. As children we loved to dream. Why stop as an adult? Keep chasing them in your adulthood. Without dreams, hope diminishes. When you dream, you become independent. It only takes "you" to reach your dreams. You don't need anyone else, you will figure it out on your own.

Dreams can also be a distraction from real life to help you get through the tough times. When you dream you are excited for the person you are and the person you will become. Dreams have no limits and you can dream as big as you want. It helps you step up your game and reach for the stars. A dream is strong enough to define who you will be in life.

Don't hold back, dream big!

Dream like you did as a child. Love like you did as a child. Play like you did as a child. Ask questions as you did as a child. Try new things as you did as a child. Live life as you did as a child. As children we were empowered and exquisite. Why lose those traits as adults?

Dreaming is powerful and so are those who dream!

Your dreams will change and grow with you as you go through life. Just remember as your dreams come true and you are moving on to new ones, don't miss the opportunity to embrace the dreams you have accomplished. This is an important part of the process. You don't want to miss these moments of realization when you did it, when you reached your dreams. You want to remember how it feels when you do. The real moment! No visualization can compare to the real thing. These are times you can reflect back when things do not go the way you expect them to go, and this is guaranteed to happen. Some of your dreams will fail, and that's life. It's how you get through those times that will determine your future experiences, as you will see later. I had to learn this the hard way.

In between the violin, but after Girl Scout cookies, came a new dream. Selling Girl Scout cookies could only get me to camp, but as I got older I wanted more. I wanted to make my own money because as a family we didn't have any. All of my friends had money as they lived across the road in Twin Lakes, a very affluent neighborhood on the golf course in Federal Way. My neighborhood was poor and so were we. At the age of 10 I was finally old enough to make my own money. You had to be 10 to work in the strawberry fields and I was all grown up and had reached the age limit. I was so excited. It was summer break and with no school, I could go to work! It felt as if this was the biggest milestone in my life. What I could do with my own money! No more jeans from Goodwill. Instead I could now buy the stylish jeans my friends had.

I can still see it clearly in my mind's eye; a school-aged girl taking a risk, calculating quickly the cost and benefit necessary to become the Strawberry Picking Season Champion. It was a hot summer in 1978 and I was riding on the bus towards Puyallup, Washington, determined to win the designation.

You see, every year hundreds of locals had the opportunity to earn money picking strawberries. It was hard and tiring work, but open to anyone, even kids, as long as they were ten years or older. It wasn't easy, and most kids that tried it would only need one day in the fields to decide it was not where they wanted to spend their summer. The bus ride alone was a deterrent. The seats were sticky and the smell of old strawberries was pretty bad. It seemed as if they waited until the end of the season to hose down the bus because the smell got worse as the season went on.

Once we got out to the fields and off the bus I would appreciate the beauty of the fields and used that to mentally put myself in a good space. I knew the day ahead was going to be long and filled with hard work. The best days were when it wasn't too hot or raining. If it rained, the fields would be muddy and I could slip, which would slow me down. If it was a hot day, the fields were even hotter as there were no trees to shade me. Seattle's weather is a coin flip, so I never knew what to expect.

We were assigned our lanes and the picking would begin. Berries were picked and placed in flats and then carried across the field to the counting area to be stacked. Payment was issued at the end of each day (a big stack of cash in my hands), based on the number of flats I filled. The berry picker who turned in the most flats at the end of the season would earn the title of Champion and receive a large monetary bonus. It was very hard work, but was one of the only ways to earn money at my age. It was surely the only way to earn the amount of money I earned, $40 to $50 a day, working from 9 a.m. to 4 p.m. but my dream was to win the Champion award and get that bonus. I wanted to win, not just for the money, but to prove to myself I COULD DO IT!

I was competing against immigrant families who were there to support their households. They had experience and high ambition levels. I remember how scratched up my arms were, how much my legs burned, and the ongoing pain to my back from bending over all day. My mom always encouraged me, telling me I had an advantage because of my fast fingers and the calluses from all the years of playing my violin. My greatest advantage as a picker in the strawberry fields was my mindset. I knew I could do it, and I was determined to win.

Well, it happened! I can't wait to tell you how I did it; how I won and took the prize. This is only half of the story. You will be surprised when I explain how I won and the strategic plan I put in place; a story shared in my professional core practice section, *Embrace Your Strengths*.

I was the #1 berry picker and named Strawberry Picking Season Champion! They gave me a very large bonus (hundreds of dollars). More importantly, I had realized my dream! I remember that day like it was yesterday, and it motivated me to pick berries the next summer, again taking the prize. I would have returned the summer after that, but it was the summer when I traveled to Europe with my violin in tow.

My success in selling Girl Scout cookies for so many years, my two summers in the strawberry fields, making it to Europe, and returning home that summer, would be the last of my successes as a young child. After returning home from Europe, at the age of 12, everything would go downhill for me and it would get really bad very quickly. That period of life marked the start of a new journey, a journey of failure,

Tina Mitchell

where I lost my belief in myself, developed a lack of confidence and lack of motivation. It took me years to get back to a place of self-assuredness, confidence, dreaming, and the motivation to work hard. It would not be until my young adult life that I would experience success again. I will explain later about my failures and the devastating life journey I took in my personal core practice section, *Learn To Fail.*

As an adult I had many more dreams that I will share in my book after uncovering my failures. Only after I explain these failures will you see why my adult dreams manifested.

Believe in yourself and you will do it!

Don't believe you can and you will fail!

Tina Mitchell

CHAPTER 2 - FINDING YOUR WHY

Do you know your "Why" behind your dream?

My Dream (is not what is important to share)

BUT

My Why (is what IS important).

My Why is "To inspire others to dream!"

The more powerful your "Why," the harder you'll fight for it.

Your "Why" is your purpose in life and is who you are. Your "Why" should not be attached to another person.

If you do what you do because of your children, try to drill it down even further than that.

- What do you want for your children?
- What do you want to see for them in this world?
- What can you do to contribute to the world they live in?

Your "Why" is your gift and part of your journey is discovering it. Once you have figured this out, everything else you do in life will be focused around sharing your gift.

Ask yourself who you are in private. It's not what you do in public that matters, but who you are in private, that shows your true self.

Gift Exercise -

Discover Your Gift, Find Your "Why" and Live Your Destiny

You were placed on this earth with a unique gift to share. Your life's purpose is to discover that gift, and to share it with the world. The world will be a better place because of you. If you don't manifest your gift and live your why the world will be missing out.

Below are a list of questions to help you discover what you are passionate about and what your gift is. This will take you to your "Why."

Don't hold back! If money and time were no object, how would you contribute to others?

- What would you do for free?
- What is important to you?
- What kind of environment do you want to live in?
- What brings you joy?
- What lights you up?
- What excites you, and gets you really fired up?
- What dreams have you talked yourself out of?

- What could you do for hours and never feel like it's work?

- Where and when do you feel most like yourself and at peace?

- What are your unique gifts and talents?

- What regrets would you have if you died tomorrow?

- Where and when are you most happy?

- What makes you feel fulfilled?

- What gives you purpose?

- What makes you laugh?

- What makes you cry? (in a good way)

- What makes you mad? (you will fight for what you believe in)

- For what do you have boundless enthusiasm?

- What is something you have done with ease your entire life?

- What did you dream about as a child?

- What is the one word others would use to describe you? (Friends, Family and Coworkers) If you ask people to describe you in one word you will see many will say the same word. I love this one and it was an enriching moment for me. It helped me to see what I already knew inside. It took this question to others to bring it to the surface for me. My word was "inspire" or "inspirational." This word took me to my "Why."

If you answer all of these, you will see a pattern. If you're not sure how to answer all of them, keep trying. Once you complete this exercise you will discover your gift, and your gift will drive your "Why."

Your gift is where your values, passions, and strengths meet. Get ready to experience a life changing moment!

What is your gift?

You may have many of the gifts listed below, but you have one gift that will shine and stand out like none of the others, just one!

Inspirer (mine)
Teacher
Listener
Connector
Creator
Motivator
Encourager
Influencer
Empathizer

Where your passion is, your heart is as well. Find your passion and you will have a happy heart and life.

You are special, you are unique and you have a gift. Embrace the real you!

CHAPTER 3 - INTENTION

"Happiness is simple. Have a dream, the **intention** to make it happen and the plan to get there."

- Tina Mitchell

It's All About Your Intention

Why do some people never reach their dreams when others do? One reason may be that they don't have the intention to make it happen. How can you make your dreams come true without intention?

You don't just start with intention. You have to build up to it and it starts with your self-talk.

Maintain a level of integrity with yourself. You can't say something you don't believe; be honest with yourself.

You have to get outside of your mind and train your thoughts. It's important to start with something you believe in. If you say "I Am" or "I Have" before you believe it, you will defeat yourself before you even get started. You have to be honest with yourself and your self-talk.

Start with something easy like "I Can." Say, "I Can Do It!" If you say "I Can" enough, it will build up to "I Will," which then builds into "I Am" or "I Have." Each step up becomes more powerful.

Once you reach the "I Am" or "I Have" level of self-talk you have the intention, and you can be or do anything, and reach any dream you have.

Intention means knowing! Knowing you "Are" or "Have" whatever your dream is. Intention is an intensely strong belief in yourself and your dream and it must be recorded.

I noticed as I got older and had more life experiences and failures, it wasn't as easy. I had to go back and start with words I could believe in, like "I Can." You will know if your words make you feel powerful or if they make you feel not worthy. Trust your feelings.

How do you practice your self-talk? Writing affirmations is one method.

When you begin, all of your affirmations should start with "I can," then they will evolve into "I will" statements and finally when that is a part of you, change them to "I Am" or "I Have" or, no verb required, as the statement just "is." I will share my affirmations at the end of this chapter.

Affirmations are intentional forms of self-talk geared to install positive messages, and our lives are byproducts of our beliefs. It's your belief that determines how you feel; your feelings will drive your actions and your actions will create the life you will live.

You can talk yourself into doing something or talk yourself out of doing something!

The majority of people will talk themselves out of something because it's easier.

Tina Mitchell

Have you noticed what always happens when you tell yourself "I'm not going to be late"? You are late! This is because your subconscious brain does not process words. The problem with negative desire statements is not that the mind can't hear or understand the negation, but that it is looking for a feeling to focus on, and uses what is given.

The reason, "I'm not going to be late" doesn't provide the result you want, is because the mind understands that you are stressed about the possibility of being late, so you will be late. Speaking of what isn't wanted only brings up the negative feelings that the mind can easily identify. If you are stressed about money, you will not have any. If you're worried about your health you can bring on health issues. Your emotions are attached to your thoughts. This is caused by the Reticular Activating System (RAS) in your brain.

The Reticular Activating System is a part of the brain that controls many things. Perhaps the most important function of the RAS is that it controls consciousness. Some say it controls sleep, wakefulness, and the ability to consciously focus on something. Others say it controls the flexibility of our behavior. Either way, it helps us to filter information in our brains. Positive affirmations allow the RAS to program our future and help us realize our dreams. Positive thoughts provoke a positive emotion. Just remember to be honest with yourself. Go with your true feelings and beliefs. Work up to the "know" and just start from the "can."

What about that ketchup bottle in the refrigerator? You tell yourself it's not there and even though you look everywhere, because of your continued conversation to yourself, "the ketchup is not in the refrigerator," you don't see it. When your husband insists it is there and comes behind you to prove it, and of course finds it, front and center, you are forced to see the truth. How did you miss it when it was right in front of your face?

You can't have your radio tuned into a rock station and expect to hear classical music. You are not tuned into the right station. There is no difference with your self talk. If you're saying discouraging things to yourself you can not produce positive results.

If you are trying to make a change in your life, from dieting to quitting smoking, you need to focus on the gain not the loss. If you are thinking about that soda you can't drink or the pizza you can't eat or you are thinking about how relaxed you would feel if only you could have a cigarette, you will eventually break down. Instead, if you're thinking about how good you will look in your new clothes from all the weight you lost or how proud you will feel being a non-smoker, the results will be completely different.

Have you seen the comical movie, Groundhog Day? While the movie is all in fun, this same scenario plays out in many lives to some extent. Think about it. Are you living the same life over and over again?

Have you noticed that the people who complain about their life the most also have the most challenges?

To change your life, you must talk to yourself differently so your life will be different. Continue saying the same things and your life will never change.

When writing affirmations, there are some very important steps to follow…

Be Strong, Powerful, Confident, Emotional, Feel Good, and Always say "I."

Affirmations are only about what you will do, not what you will do for someone else or what someone else will do for you.

Remember you are only in control of your life, not someone else's life.

Affirmations are meant to develop belief in you!

Find your own way to express your affirmations…

Write them, sing them, shout out, record your own voice and listen, or say them into a mirror. You will find the way that works best for you.

If you say "I can," you will. If you say "I can't," you won't.

We get to choose the words we say to ourselves. Choose wisely!

If you want to be like the majority, do what the majority does. If you want to be special, do things differently. Talk to yourself differently and bring your gift to the surface. We all have a gift to give to others. Part of your journey is to find out what your gift is and to share it with the world.

Don't worry about what others say to you, worry about what you say to yourself. Believe in yourself and others will believe in you. Motivate yourself and you will motivate others. Be inspirational and you will inspire others.

I have always heard to treat others like you want to be treated. I think this is backwards. I believe I need to treat myself like I would treat any other person I care about. Treat yourself like you would treat anyone else you love. You have to be good to yourself before you can be good to anyone else! Love is within you. It starts inside you first! Hug yourself, praise yourself and encourage yourself. Only after loving yourself can you truly be loving to others.

Your self-talk matters and it takes practice! Ask yourself how you talk to yourself... Would you talk to someone you care about like this? Would you talk to someone you don't care about like this? Why do you say these words to yourself?

Once you have the intention to make your dream happen, you want to dream the end and experience how it feels and looks. Don't get stuck in the how or in the middle. It doesn't matter how, as long as you believe you will get there. Go ahead and dream...

You know how people refer to sleeping as falling asleep? Well, I believe that occasionally you can fall into a dream, too. For this to happen, you have to already have the intention related to the topic.

Tina Mitchell

My Affirmations...

I make every day a great day.
I have an abundance of energy today.
I am full of positive thoughts.
I have peace and fulfillment.
I am grateful for everything I have.
I live in the moment.
I am alive, excited and full of energy.
I choose to be the best at what I do.
I am a positive thinker.
My actions conquer any fear I have.
I believe in myself.
I do anything I set my mind to do.
I have complete control over my future.
I am deeply fulfilled by all that I do.
I attract positive people and things in my life.
I have complete control over my future.
I am 100% committed to my success.
I am easily motivated by my thoughts.
I love and accept myself just the way I am.
I listen with love to my body's messages.
I trust my inner wisdom.
I choose to make my life an amazing one.
Every experience is a success.
My destiny is by choice not by chance.
At the end of the day I have no regrets.
I am healthy, whole and complete.
My life is filled with joy, faith and love.
I act on my dreams.
I have a message to share and I am sharing it with the world.
I live up to my potential each and every day.
Each day brings wonderful new surprises.
I love my life!
I love myself!
Today is going to be an amazing day!

These are my affirmations and what I say every morning as loudly as I can while the Rocky Theme song is blasting through my headphones in the background. I really get into the moment! What a power tool it has been for me! My affirmations have assisted me in building my intention to the highest level so I can live my life to the fullest and reach my dreams!

Affirmations are powerful!

CHAPTER 4 - HAVE "A" PLAN

"Happiness is simple. Have a dream, the intention to make it happen and **a plan** to get there."

> **- Tina Mitchell**

Plan – Have "A" Plan not "The" Plan

"The" plan means it has to be the right plan and doesn't give you permission to fail. However, "A" plan means you will be working towards your dream and giving yourself permission to fail. If it's not the right plan you will figure it out and find the right one.

The fun in life is seeing what's going to happen next. How is your plan going to turn out? Also a plan is just part of the journey. Life is about the journey not the destination. Enjoy the ride of life and learn from it.

What do you do when a plan fails? You go back and track what parts of the plan worked and what parts of the plan failed. The whole plan was not a loss, only components of it. Look back and pull out all the components that worked and implement them into your new plan.

Steve Jobs gave a commencement speech for Stanford where he urged students and faculty to "connect the dots." Jobs talks about not knowing if, when or how the dots will connect, but stresses the need to just trust that they will.

I think part of the fun in life is trying to guess where the dots will connect and being able to reflect back to see if you were right or wrong. It doesn't matter if they connect or not, as long as you are not attached to the outcome. Just know that some things will work out and others will not. However, if you don't have a plan, nothing of substance will ever result.

Remember the last chapter, "Intention." If you don't have a plan, how can you have the intention to reach your goal? You need all three… A dream, the intention and a plan. Just "a" plan, not "the" plan!

Just saying you will have a million dollars doesn't mean you will have it. It doesn't matter how many times you repeat it or visualize it. Maybe you will be one of the few that it just falls into your lap, but for most of us this will not happen. You have to work hard to get what you want in life, and without a plan or a roadmap it's almost impossible to get there.

If you were traveling across the country on a road trip and you had no navigation or a map, it would be pretty stressful if you didn't know where you were going. But with navigation or a map (a plan) it makes the journey easier, more enjoyable and you have a much better chance of success.

Have you noticed with most people that when "luck" comes into play, the success is not usually sustainable. Look at the statistics of people who have won the lottery. The National Endowment for Financial Education points to research that estimates 70 percent of people would have been much better off never winning the lottery at all.

The important thing to know is that if your plan fails and you have to start over, you are not starting from the beginning; you are just starting from where you left off. Look at all you learned from your journey so far. If you had never started the plan, you would have not taken away the knowledge. A saying I have heard and love is, "fail forward." Learn from your failure, but don't focus on it. Focusing on them, will only bring more failure, but learning from them will make you stronger moving forward.

Steps To Take

1. Write your dream down!
Be as detailed and specific as you can about your dream. What does it look like, smell like, taste like, and most importantly, how do you feel when you have realized it?

2. Visualize it!
Work on all or some of the techniques I shared with your earlier.

3. Believe it!
Remember my chapter entitled, "Intention"? This is one of the steps to build your belief in yourself and your dream. All the steps below will not matter if you don't believe you can do it.

4. Write your "why" behind your dream.
Remember if your "why" is big enough you will do everything necessary to reach your dream. You will fight for it!

5. Plan the steps.
There are many ways to get to your dream. Make a list of each one of the steps and the order you would like to work on them. It's important to prioritize, work on one step at a time, and follow "a" plan.

6. Set a deadline.
Having a deadline is important so you are working towards your dream with urgency. It's okay if the deadline has to be extended, but always have one. Try to set a realistic deadline because it's always better to be

ahead than to have to extend, but at the same time, don't make it too easy for yourself. You want your deadline to challenge you and to keep a sense of urgency.

7. Review your progress on a regular basis.

Once a week, biweekly or once a month, depending on what it is. Are you meeting the deadlines you set up for each step? This will keep you on track.

8. Monitor.

Monitoring what's working and what's not working is an important part of the process. Make sure you allow enough time for fine-tuning the steps that are not working to ensure you don't give up too soon. You don't want to dismiss something that just needs a little tweaking.

9. Keep the end in sight.

Work on one step at a time and don't allow yourself to get stuck in the middle. You should just have the end in sight and work on the task at hand. If you worry about everything it will take to reach your dream, you may defeat yourself before you get the opportunity to realize it.

10. Don't take short cuts.

Remember this is a dream, a big dream, and you have to go through the process to obtain it. Remember the lottery winners?

11. Be Patient.

Greatness doesn't happen quickly. You must be patient.

An inspiration for me is the Chinese Bamboo Tree. I consider <u>Water The Bamboo</u> by Greg Bell a must read. It takes 5 years for the Chinese Bamboo tree to grow. It has to be watered and fertilized every day and yet it doesn't break through the ground until the fifth year. However, once it breaks through, in 6 weeks it grows 90 feet tall. If you stop at any time from watering and fertilizing it, it will die. Every drop of water makes a difference. What was happening for all those years? Under the ground, an enormous network of roots was developing to support the Bamboo's sudden growth.

Most great things in life don't happen overnight. You have to give it time and be patient. Believe in yourself and continue to take the steps necessary to accomplish what you want in life.

Take for instance the example of lottery winners. Many had no support to hold them up when they suddenly won and they found themselves flooded with money. How could they be prepared for that drastic change in their life? Big dreams take time to realize and this time gives you what you need so you can be prepared when you reach your dreams.

We have all seen people who have had quick success in life, such as young movie stars or athletes. We witness many of them failing in other areas of their lives, getting into drugs and making other bad decisions. Why is this? It is because they don't have their foundation or roots yet.

Remember what is happening under the surface. Sometimes you just have to wait to see the results. If you give up too soon, your tree or dream will die.

12. Last step - Enjoy it!

Once you reach your dream, remember to enjoy the moment. It is the real moment and you don't want to miss a second of it. You created it and you want to remember how it felt and use this feeling as your trigger to manifest your next dream. When you have failure trying to reach your dream, reflect back to the feeling you had when you made progress on another step and remember how that success felt. It will help you move forward and help you not to give up.

Ask yourself every day "who am I and who do I want to be?" And then ask yourself "do they align?"

Tina Mitchell

CHAPTER 5 - BE ALERT

"Wake up every morning alert to all the surprises waiting just for you. They show up everywhere when you're watching for them and what an amazing day it will be!"

- Tina Mitchell

Be alert to the small miracles and they will manifest every day, all day long. Focus on all the good and beautiful things that make you happy. You will always have something to smile about if you are alert to the small things. Wait for the big miracles and you may be waiting a long time.

For me a few are…

▸ **An animal**

A dog walking with its owner or a dog's smiling face peeking outside the window of a traveling car.

▸ **A mother and her child**

A mother playing with her child in the park or a special moment you are blessed to see between the two of them.

▸ **A child's magical view on life**

Children are happy, confident and loving and have a way of making everything around them so special.

‣ Nature

I love all aspects of nature, from the rain after a few dry days to the different fragrances of flowers in a garden, from the damp earth and smell of old fallen leaves in the woods, to the fresh smell of a lake or salty smell of the ocean. I love stepping on crisp leaves and admiring the pine trees in Seattle.

Nature is all around you and brings magical feelings if you take time to stop for a moment and embrace it!

‣ A stranger holding the door open for me

I love it when someone I don't know makes this kind gesture and holds the door open and a small smile is exchanged between the two of us.

‣ Someone letting me over in traffic

When someone makes an extra special effort to let me over in traffic on a busy highway, this gesture of kindness can make my day. I always embrace the moment and the feeling I get when I look back in my rear view mirror, smiling as I give a wave showing my appreciation.

‣ When a stranger smiles at me

This always makes me feel good and by being alert to that smile, that smile can change my day!

These are just a few small things that give me warm and fuzzy feelings. I encourage you to embrace the small special surprises waiting just for you. Many people will let them pass without embracing them and even worse, not noticing them at all. If you miss them, you will not experience the compound magical effect they will have on you.

Today will be what you make of it!

Tina Mitchell

Do you want just a great day or a great year or do you want a great life?

When embracing these moments I naturally become a better person to others. I want to make others feel as good as they make me feel. I find myself doing for others what makes me feel good. Isn't life wonderful?

We get to choose if we want to do for others or do for ourselves. The act of kindness to others is where true happiness exists.

How wonderful it feels to be good to someone else. You never know how the small gestures you make to a stranger may affect their day, and just maybe even their life depending on the space they are in. A good day when having a bad one can also have a compound effect and make a true difference in their future experience just based on that one gesture of kindness you showed them. You never know!

One of my favorite things to do in a parking lot is to look for the best space, manifest someone behind me, and waive them into that spot. It feels so good and always puts me in a good mood, no matter what's going on in my own life at that moment.

Another thing I love to do (just as I mentioned above that I love when people do for me)... when I'm on a busy highway, I always watch for someone trying to get over in traffic so I can let them in. When I don't notice and pass them, then realize what I did, I feel so bad I missed this opportunity. I have a funny story I have to share. My husband Dave has the biggest heart and would do anything for anyone he knows, but for some strange reason when he is on the road, he has no patience.

He will step on the gas pedal when he notices someone trying to change lanes. One day when we were driving together I had to ask him why. I said, "Dave, why is it that you never let anyone over in traffic?

Does that make you feel good?" He responded back, "If I let everyone over like you do, no one would ever get to where they are trying to go." He continued to say, "I know we need drivers like you, because if they all drove like me no one would get anywhere either. Just as you always say, 'life is balanced.' We need both types of drivers." We laughed together. Isn't that the truth? Everything is balanced, even people on the road and how they drive, is a balancing act. You will see what I mean when you read the chapter on my personal core practice, *Learn To Fail*.

If I'm having a challenging day, I like to stop and embrace the good feelings I have as I assist someone else. It changes my outlook and I feel less connected to whatever I thought was challenging.

Live your life for today, not for tomorrow or yesterday. Live your life for this moment and embrace every moment in your life.

Live in the now and today, not the later or tomorrow.

The majority of people hold their happiness hostage by waiting for the miracles in life. Choose to embrace happiness by being alert to all the small things around you and create your own miracles.

I appreciate the small things in life, a quality I received from my mom. At a young age I was embarrassed by my mom but, as an adult, I realized what a special and beautiful person she really is.

I want to share two stories about my mom so you, too, will see how special and beautiful she is. She's a little quirky too!

Tina Mitchell

My mom loves all the small things in life and made every moment more special than it may have been. She makes every second of her day matter just as I do now as an adult.

When I was a fill-in manager at Denny's restaurant my mom was so proud of me. She always was. She wanted to support me and be a part of everything I did. You know how much my mom loves trains? Well, she belonged to a train club. Almost all the people who were part of this club had a lot of money and traveled all over the U.S. by train. My mom could not afford to do this, but her friends from the train club would bring her back buttons and patches from their travels, because she collected them.

Every Saturday my mom would go to the train club and beforehand, she would stop into the Denny's I worked at, not to see me, because by the time she got there my shift was already over. She went just because it was my store and she wanted to support me.

She would come in all decked out (I wish I had a picture to show you). It was priceless. She came fully dressed in her train conductor attire. You know the black and white overalls? She came with the conductor hat and all. She probably found her outfit during one of her great finds at Goodwill, her favorite store. Not only was she in the conductor uniform but she also had every single button and patch that her train club friends had brought her back from their travels. She was literally head to toe in buttons and patches. Can you imagine what the waitresses said about her? You would be correct. They called my mom "the train lady" and not in a very nice way. No one was excited to wait on her, because she didn't have a lot of money to tip, and she would take all the extra creams and sugars. I said she was quirky, right? Resourceful, too!

One Saturday morning I happened to still be at the restaurant. It was 7:00 a.m. and my shift had run late, because the night before one of my cooks didn't show up for work. I was on the cook's line all night helping with the orders, and by the time my mom arrived I was just finishing up the till and the scheduling responsibilities I had.

I saw my mom in the corner table and went to sit down and have a cup of coffee with her. When I walked back to the servicer's station where all the waitresses were, one of them said, "You know the train lady???" in a rude tone as the others laughed. I responded proudly, with a smile and said, "Yes, that's my mom!" You can only imagine how embarrassed they were after being so cruel in their response.

To know my mom, to truly know her, is to love her.

Another story I would like to share...

As an adult a few years ago, I was strolling in downtown Redmond, Washington at the Redmond Town Center, a very ritzy part of town where you could spend a good deal of money shopping. As I was walking I saw two older very well dressed women (around my mom's age) walking their basset hound dogs. I had to stop to say hi and pet their dogs. I said, "My mom loves basset hounds and has two of her own." I asked if I could pet them and they graciously said, "Of course, yes." I was loving on their dogs as I started to tell a story about my mom.

I was sharing with them how my mom always went to these events that were sponsored by Puget Sound Basset Rescue where they would bring their dogs, and I went on to explain how cute I thought it was that everyone would show their dogs dressed up in costume, while my mom would be the only owner who actually dressed herself up too. She handmade both her dogs and her costume to match. She was the only owner to be in costume at all, and to boot she matched her dogs. One of the women said in a very friendly way, "Oh my gosh, is your mom Beth Samuelson?" I proudly said, "Yes, that's my mom." All three of us had a special laugh together, a laugh that only we could experience and enjoy because we have the privilege to know my mom and know how special she is. What a surprisingly unexpected day! I ran into these two women in Redmond, Washington, a very different world from my mom who live in Elbe, Washington.

I often think of these moments and smile!

I am so proud to call my mom, my mom and I'm grateful of how I love the little things in life because I am her daughter. What a special gift she gave me.

How beautiful life is!

I tell myself every morning, "my life is beautiful and so is everything in it!"

You will be a happier person if you, like my mom, can focus on what feels good. Just focusing on the small things in life can make all the difference in how you feel. How you feel will make all the difference in how you treat others. How you treat others will determine your happiness in life.

It's okay to want more out of life, but it's important to love the life you have now and accept where you are at in your life. Don't live your life wanting more, but instead love your life and strive to be more.

The possibilities in life are endless when you make the decision to be happy!

Your attitude will create your reality. You can't work on being greater than how you feel. Instead, work on how you feel and get greater at life. Happiness doesn't exist in the future. Your state of happiness is your today and your tomorrow.

Your body has an internal navigation system that tells you what feels good. Pay attention and be alert to those feelings! Being alert is understanding your body. Pay attention to what your body is telling you feels good.

Wake up every morning alert to all the surprises waiting just for you and make the decision to recognize them. You will have a better day and a better life!

Once you recognize these feelings, these moments will come more frequently.

When you don't feel good, draw from one of your "positive triggers" (a place where you did feel good), and focus your attention on that place or feeling. By being alert to all the small things that make you feel good, you can easily look around and reach for one of them.

Be happy for what you have now instead of waiting to have something to make you happy. You have to make the decision to be happy in order to attract things in your life.

You can't shut off your negative thoughts, but you can make the decision to focus only on your positive ones.

You can't shut off the negative people, but you can choose how you react to them.

Choose to come from a place of love, acceptance and accountability.

Love is being genuine and real. Acceptance is welcoming that person regardless of the way they are treating you. Accountability is taking responsibility for your part in the relationship.

The people who seem to trigger the most negative feelings are the people we are closest to and love the most. Why is that? Because we are around them all the time, we don't give them as much slack and more often we will take advantage of that relationship.

I can give you an example. My husband Dave!

After being married for many years and going through the ups and downs that we all do (because as life, our relationships, too, are balanced), I made a conscious decision to see if I could improve our relationship by reacting differently when I felt he was being mean or unfair to me. I decided the next time this happened that instead of reacting I would go to one of my "Dave Trigger" places. These are good feelings I have about him... why I love him.

Most people associate triggers with negative memories. Why not reflect on your positive triggers? They too are there if you watch for them. Intentionally create positive triggers you can reflect back on when things are hard and unfair, as these times are guaranteed to show up. The first opportunity I had to test it, I thought I would go all out and I shot for the biggest trigger I could think of!

Here it is…The trigger like no other. My Dave trigger!

I was only 26 when I met Dave and we started dating. When you are young you may make relationship commitments that later you realize you can not live up to. This was the case for me. Dave had already been married as I had and he already had a daughter, Stephanie. He is eight years older than me and he didn't want any more children. I made the commitment out of love for him that I would be okay not having any children of my own. Years later this was a decision that would bring me great pain and stress in my life. There were times when I questioned everything I was and everything I had given up to be with Dave. I focused on the loss in my marriage and not the gain of having Dave in my life. Ten years into our married life, I made the decision to walk away from our marriage in 2004 at 36 years old.

When I decided to give our marriage another try 6 months after leaving him, we hired a marriage counselor. After a few months of weekly visits and one on one visits separately with our counselor, during one of our couples sessions our counselor said she was no longer going to counsel us and she had to let us go. The way I heard it, she just fired us! I know crazy, right? I couldn't understand why. Dave and I both were showing up every week and showing up on time. Not only that, we were doing all the exercises she gave us to do. We were having date nights and working on our communication skills... you get the gist. I thought it was ludicrous that she was letting us go.

She went on to explain that we were wasting her time and wasting our money because if continued down the path we were on, our marriage was guaranteed to end in a divorce. She went on to further explain that the one area where she said we needed most improvement was our careers. She suggested that we both make our marriage our priority, not our careers. She explained that even with all the exercises and time we were spending to improve our marriage, it really was not going to solve our problem because we were not willing to do the one big thing. We were not willing to sacrifice our careers to make more time for our marriage.

I was shocked. She wanted me to sacrifice my career? My career was all I had since I had no biological children. I did have my stepdaughter Stephanie, but only during the Christmas holidays and summer vacations, since she was in another state. I was just a part-time mom and what else did I have but my career when Stephanie was not around? This was what I was thinking. I was not willing to make my marriage my priority because my career took center stage. My career was my identity. It made me who I was. What would I have if I sacrificed it? You may be thinking this was selfish and to be honest with you, it was. I really did have a great husband.

I realized after listening to her, we were willing to work on the small things, but not the one big thing. We were willing to do what was easy but not the one difficult thing.

Do you know those people in life that you will forever thank? Well, our marriage counselor was one of them. Dave and I both tried to remember who she was to go back years later and thank her, but to no avail. She made me think... Was my marriage worth it? Was it more important than just a career? Back in these earlier years I had not yet got to the place of reflection and appreciation that I am today, so I allowed time to pass without connecting, and now the opportunity, I'm afraid, is lost. To this day, she may not even know that she played an instrumental role in saving our marriage.

Dave and I both left after that last session in disbelief. There was no conversation to be had after we returned home. It was a Thursday night and late. We both had a long day ahead of us and just went to bed. Friday came and went and still there was no conversation about the session. It was now Saturday and both of us were home. This rarely happened as I was always teaching first time home buyer seminars and Dave would normally have been at the huge job he was running as a Commercial Superintendent for GLY Construction. That day, though, both of us were home and neither one of us knew that the other one was taking the day off. We both had covered our responsibilities and needed some quiet time to think.

We had too much going on in our heads to focus on work and it was time to reflect. The day turned into an intense conversation on what we were going to do to save our marriage. I suggested maybe I quit the mortgage industry and come to work for the company he worked for. After all, I had great marketing skills and it wasn't like I had never changed careers before. Maybe I could market for new business for GLY so we would be together. Dave suggested maybe he quit the construction industry and join me as a member of my team in my mortgage practice and we could be together. Well, that's what happened. After almost 30 years in the construction industry, in 2005 after that one intense conversation the next working day (Monday) he gave the owners of GLY notice.

He gave it all up to come work for me. He gave up his entire career to be an employee of his wife. He became part of my success, leaving his own success behind. He never looked back and we have now been married for 20 years. Dave explained to me that since I had sacrificed having children of my own, he was willing to make the sacrifice this time giving up his career to put me first, allowing me to keep mine.

This was my "Dave Trigger."

Years later when I made the decision to work on our relationship and come from a place of love, acceptance and accountability, you might image what happened. The next time he was mean and unfair to me, I reflected back to my "Dave Trigger." Of course, I cried! I couldn't believe how I had reacted to him in the past. I was just as guilty as he was. I was mean and unfair, too.

When we change how we react to someone and come from a place of love, acceptance and accountability they will react differently. I have to admit I don't always go to my positive triggers because sometimes I just want to react, because I'm not perfect, but most of the time I do try.

You can turn anger into compassion if you allow yourself to move through it. Test this with someone you are close to. You will see it feels beautiful and your relationship with that person will never be the same!

If this exercise doesn't work, then maybe the relationship is not the right one. You will only know if you give it all you can, but if you don't, you may lose a great one. Give it everything you have without expecting anything in return. You will be surprised with the results if you go for it, and go for it with an open heart and require nothing.

Sometimes you need to fight for what is right and you will know those times, but most of the time it's just your ego talking. Be intentional in your interactions with others and recognize how you react, it will have an impact on your communication and your relationships.

Live to be a good person not wanting other people to be good to you first.

Dave has now retired but we worked together for 9 years and it completely changed our marriage. We went from spending no time together to spending all our time together. We went from embracing our own individual successes and challenges to embracing our success as one unit and dealing with our challenges as a team. We were partners in marriage and partners in business. I did remain the boss, but Dave gladly allowed me to keep center stage and he took back stage because he loves me. This is what marriage is all about. Both individuals compromising and making sacrifices for the betterment of the relationship. THANK YOU, DAVE! I LOVE YOU!

You can't change others, but you can change yourself, and others will react differently to you when you do.

Be the best you and you will be better to others.

Tina Mitchell

CHAPTER 6 - EMBRACE YOUR DAY

Do you hit the snooze button? If you do, you are telling yourself you're not excited about your life and what the day has to offer. Live every second of your day. Don't waste a moment!

Are you sleeping to renew yourself or sleeping to avoid the day?

Look in the mirror. Who do you see? Do you see sadness, anger and fear or do you see happiness, lovingness and confidence? Be strong and ready to conquer the day.

How you start and end your day is important to your success.

In the morning when you wake up - Be Thankful & Get Motivated. Use Your Affirmations!

This is the time of the day for "motivation" because it's the start of the day and you have to get ready for it! Life rules guarantee something will not go your way. However motivation brings strength and the will to help you overcome any challenge that may arise.

Many people watch the news first thing in the morning and it is not the ideal way to start your day! It's not a very motivating start! If you need to watch the news, the best time to do so is when you get home from work as long as you have a few hours left before you go to bed. I'm in the mortgage industry, work with powerful people, host a radio show and I don't watch the news. I read what I need to know on-line and that is enough. I get to choose what I read and where I focus my attention.

My Morning Routine…

I start my day with what I am thankful for then I listen to my favorite motivation clips while I'm getting ready in the morning and continue listening on my drive to work. I have hours of them in my rotation. I have received the most motivation from Les Brown and Eric Thomas. I can listen to either of them for hours. I end my morning routine with my affirmations that I shared earlier. I wait to do my affirmations until I get into my office as I am the first one there so I can shout them as loud as I like and no one can hear me. I wait until I get to my office so as not to lose the momentum I receive from doing this exercise. It brings on the power and strength I need to conquer my day!

During my *Live Your Dream Now* workshop I always share my affirmations while blasting the Rocky theme song, saying them along as loud as I can just as I do in the morning. I ask the audience to participate with me. Afterwards, I will ask them, "How did that make you feel?... awkward or amazing?" If amazing, I then will advise them to write and start doing their own affirmations at the first opportunity they have to do so. If the answer is awkward, I will then advise them to do something different to get motivated!

What's motivating for me may not be motivating for you, and that is okay. What's important is that you embrace something, something that feels good to you, not because it is working for someone else. You will know what feels right when you do it. Go with your first impulse. If you have to force it, it's not for you and it will never work. It actually can do the exact opposite and you are better off not doing anything at all. Which is not what you want, so find what motivates you, embrace it and just do it! Remember what I mentioned earlier; the brain only knows the emotion behind the words, not the words themselves.

Tina Mitchell

Be who you are meant to be. Don't try to be someone you are not.

At night before you go to bed – Be Thankful, Reflect & Get Inspired. Journal and Visualize!

Nighttime is the very end of the day and it's time to wrap it up. It's time to go to bed and dream. You don't want to get motivated before you go to sleep; you want to get inspired, so that you have quiet and calming things to dream about. Can you imagine screaming affirmations to the Rocky Theme song then trying to go to sleep?

My Evening Routine...

Journaling is especially good at night. First, on the right hand side of my journal I write what I am thankful for that day. On the left hand side of my journal, I write what I thought the day's challenges were. I do this while listening to my favorite inspirational music – not motivation but inspiration. It's important to take note of both, the good and the bad. The reason to cite both good and bad is because an important part of your journey is to go back and see how things played out. Remember what Steve Jobs talked about regarding "connecting the dots." Some things you may have thought were challenges may have turned out to be positive, life-changing events, or events which connected to something else that was monumental. If you are not writing them down, you may miss this realization. The other important part of this process is that it will naturally change your thoughts regarding your challenges, because you will start to recognize that later you can reflect back and see if you were correct or not. I love it when I'm wrong!

If you don't journal in complete sentences, don't worry - you can just bullet point. This is what I do because I am not into journaling sentences (I know it's a little strange because I wrote this book).

Isn't it fun to turn negative into positive?

If you have not picked up the book *The Miracle Morning: The Not-So-Obvious Secret Guaranteed To Transform Your Life... Before 8AM* by Hal Elrod, it is a must read. Hal shares his inspiring life journey of how he died at age 20. He was hit head on by a drunk driver at 70 mph, broke 11 bones, died for 6 minutes, and spent 6 days in a coma only to wake up to face the news that he may never walk again...

Not only did Hal walk, he went on to run a 52-mile ultra marathon. You might think this was the moment that would change his life but Hal explains in his book that the real moment was yet to come. Years later Hal lost almost everything he had earned. He lost his house; went from the best shape of his life 5.7% body to 17% body fat and from debt free to accruing $53k in credit card debt. Instead of letting this take him down, he fought, and fought hard. He would not only change his life by creating the "Miracle Morning" but after sharing it, over 100,000 others are doing the "Miracle Morning" and changing their lives as well.

I have an extra special connection to Hal because he and I were affected by the same tragedy; the financial meltdown. At the same time and for the same reason, my life changed due to the 2008 financial meltdown which I will share later. Hal shares a list of morning rituals that he created for himself to overcome any challenges, and you too can use them to overcome any challenges you are facing today. Hal's book will transform your life.

Tina Mitchell

We have routines for our external selves – groom ourselves, brush our teeth and take a shower.

Why not have routines for our internal selves (how we feel inside)?

Case in point: If your car runs out of gas, you fill it up.

Why not fill up your personal gas tank?

Another scenario: You take your car in for a tune up on a regular basis.

Why not have continued maintenance and tune yourself up on a personal level?

One more checkpoint: When driving somewhere and your navigation system says you have taken a wrong road, you redirect.

Our body has a navigational system – Are you taking time to listen and respond?

Speaking of navigational systems, I spend a lot of my time in my car. It's almost a sacred space to me as I cruise down the road, listening to inspiring talks or songs. I can blast my motivational music in my car or listen to my favorite motivational speakers. This is my time and my space to do anything I want. I can embrace whatever feels good at the moment, with no interruptions, and I have experienced so many magical moments. I know it may seem strange but my car is the place where a lot of great ideas are sparked. I have to share one of those moments with you. It came when I wrote my song "Dream."

This is what's magical about being alert to what your body is telling you. When you get that warm and fuzzy feeling inside, it's your body telling you to STOP and embrace. Hold on because something great is happening. If you don't embrace it, it will come and go very quickly and the moment may never come again. But if you stop and see where it's taking you, you may just experience something that will change your life and possibly change your life forever.

I have experienced many of these moments and would like to share one of them.

As I was driving, I noticed all these words were going through my head. Not just normal words, these words were special. I could feel it! "Live your dream now. Sing, dance and play." These were just a few of the words that were going on in my head. I didn't know why but I felt that warm and fuzzy feeling. As I embraced that feeling, I felt goose bumps, quickly followed by tears of joy. I was on the I-5 freeway heading home from a long day at the office. I immediately pulled over to the side of the freeway and pulled out my little black book (the book I had in my purse just for this reason, to capture any thoughts that came up). However, these were not just words; they were something much more than that. I scribbled down in my book as quickly as I could so as not to forget the words. I wrote down the words I was feeling in that moment, "warm and fuzzy, goosebumps and tears of joy."

When I got home I called my friend Stephanie McCarthy, and said "I think I just wrote a poem. May I share it with you?" Being my best friend and knowing me as well as she does, she said, "Yes, of course." As I read the words to her I cried and she teared up with me. I still am not sure if she was emotional with me because of the words or just because she knew how important they were to me. That was in July of 2014. As we ended the phone call, I said "I think I will name my poem 'Dream'." We hung up the phone, and I was not to read those words again until a year later.

Tina Mitchell

One year after that moment in the car, I was asked to share my workshop, *Live Your Dream Now* at the House of Hope. I was sharing it with women who needed my message and were staying at the home. It was a chance to live my purpose, and inspire others to dream. This would be my first of many more to come; visits with homeless women where I had the honor to speak with them.

The House of Hope is an extension of Mamma's Hands, and is an organization based in Western Washington, dedicated to feeding the homeless on the streets of Seattle (Mamma's Hands) and helping the homeless women and their children get a fresh start (House of Hope). They provide a safe and secure 24-hour living environment for women and children in crisis, including workshops and lessons on how to get back on track.

I knew I couldn't just share my workshop in the same way I had with mortgage and real estate professionals, but that I was going to have to get personal. How could I drive up to their home in my Jaguar and talk to them about the importance of having a dream when they were just trying to get back on their own and provide a home (their own home) for their children? This was such an important opportunity for me and I didn't want to blow it. When would I have an opportunity like this again, to share my message with women who really could benefit from it in a big way? How was I going to make an impact on their lives without sharing my personal story, my whole story? I couldn't think of a way to avoid it. So I did; I shared extremely personal details of my life.

I shared my childhood. I talked about my dad. I talked about my mom and playing my violin on the street at Pike Place Market. I talked about the loss of my daughter, and how my first husband was in prison for many years. (I will share later with you the story of my daughter,

Amber, and my first husband, Mike). I shared all my successes and all my failures. It was so empowering for me and was an inspiration for the women. This was the first time I had ever shared publicly about my personal challenges.

I shared about my need to dream and I shared how visualization brought all the goodness I experience today in my life. I talked about their community and how they, as women, could draw strength from one another.

I shared about failure and loss and how they, too, could beat what life was throwing at them!

I shared about passion, reflection, inspiration and motivation. I challenged each of them to find one thing that they could improve and help one another with. I challenged them to share it with the group and to keep each other accountable. Remarkably, they did and none of the women said the same thing! It was a memorable moment and a bonding experience for all of us! It was a night I will never forget.

After spending three hours with the women I knew I helped them and that my life was forever changed. When I left the house, I was walking out to my car wishing I had something to leave with the women, something they could go back to, to remember the special time we had spent together as I didn't know if I would ever see them again, but I didn't have anything.

As soon as I opened the door to get into my car. I suddenly thought, 'Dream'! That's why I wrote that poem, it wasn't meant to be a poem at all; it was meant to be a song. A song I can share with others to help them during tough times.

When the women are feeling down, here was a song, which just maybe would create a safe space for them the dream, work on their recovery and get back on their feet!

The next time I visited the House of Hope I shared my song, "Dream" with the women and they embraced it. To this day, when someone is having a bad day I will share my song in hopes it will help them as well.

There have been many scientific studies that show when you sing, musical vibrations move through you, altering your physical and emotional landscape. The joy comes from endorphins, hormones released by singing, hormones that are associated with feelings of pleasure. Oxytocin, another hormone released during singing, has been found to ease anxiety and stress. Oxytocin also enhances feelings of trust and bonding.

If you are depressed, stressed, feeling lonely, or have any feeling of sadness, singing will change your mood. I loved learning this because now I understand why music touches me so much, adding to the musical experiences I had as a child.

Thank you to all the women at the House of Hope and its founders Denny and Leslie Hancock for inviting me to share. Because of you, 'Dream' came alive and because of you, I have published my book. I came to be an inspiration to you, and you were all an inspiration to me. Isn't life spectacular!

See how the smallest thought can turn into the biggest life change. As I stated earlier, I spoke with the women at the House of Hope in July of 2015, and I am now writing my book in November of 2015, and will be published in the first half of 2016. Some things, even big things can move very quickly if you just embrace the moment.

If you don't embrace these moments, you will not grow. If you do embrace them, I believe you continue to stretch your feeling of happiness to higher levels. When you study, you get smarter and will never go backwards in your knowledge. When you embrace your happiness, you go to new heights of happiness and you will never go back. You have trained your subconscious and are now a stronger person. Don't miss out on this realization. It will change your LIFE as it has mine! Embrace every moment of happiness and see how far it will take you!

I am now sharing my *Live Your Dream Now* workshop with The Hoff Foundation and Esther's Place, providing support for the homeless. Their motto is "Transforming Communities One Person at a Time." I love this motto. We can all live life to help one person at a time. Make a difference in one, and see how it will expand to many. Hearing their motto has changed my self talk. Instead of saying, "I will inspire the world," I say, " I will inspire one person today."

I have also just been invited to share my message with Mary's Place, in the Family Center. This organization offers emergency shelter to families; mom, dad and children all get to stay together. These families have not yet made it into transitional housing but are still living on the street. Mary's Place provides beds for the family and helps them move on to transitional housing. Mary's Place provides resources for them, and I am honored to be one of those resources. I will be speaking with the parents every month and sharing my message to Dream, Be Alert and Learn to Fail.

We have so much to learn from one another and we have so much to give to one another!

Tina Mitchell

Take control of your life, don't let life control you.

Be happy in this moment and see how you can alter your future moments!

Ordinary moments become defining moments if you embrace them. Think about what you may miss if you don't.

My song "Dream" is found on the next page. "Dream" would not have been possible without the help of a brilliant team. Thank you, Dan Wingard for management, Brian Monroney for arrangement and instruments and for being engineer and producer, Emily McIntosh for vocals, and Ann Marie Gill for creating the "Dream" video. You all made my song "Dream" come alive! THANK YOU!

You can search the song, Dream by Tina Mitchell on YouTube.

Tina Mitchell

"Dream"

I will not miss a moment. I listen, watch and feel.
The day is filled with miracles. My dream is real.

How beautiful I am. How wonderful the world around me.
I feel the joy in my heart. And my dream surrounds me.

Chorus
I open my eyes, then open my heart.
I feel the magic inside and that's how I start.

My life is now, every second of the day.
I live my dream now. I sing, dance and play.
I live my dream now. I sing, dance and play.
I live my dream now.

I watch and listen closely to see. All that life's meant to be.
The beauty shines so bright. As I smile through this journey called life.

Chorus

I'll make the difference I was meant to make. I'll leave the legacy I was
meant to leave.
I live my life and give to others. I will not waste this gift I was given.

Chorus

I listen to how my body talks. It tells me how I feel.
Goosebumps and tears of joy comes a light so bright.
The warm and fuzzy feeling inside. Is when everything's so right.

I sing dance and play.
I sing dance and play.
Live your dream now.

Listen to the full version of Dream on YouTube.

Look up "Dream" by Tina Mitchell

Tina Mitchell

CHAPTER 7 - THE REFLECTION CHALLENGE

The Reflection Challenge has been designed for reflection and self-growth. Use this challenge as a tool to enrich your life and others around you. Create a happy and peaceful journey for you, and it will change your life and the lives of others.

Work on your life not just in it! What can you do to change the world?

Take the 30 day Reflection Challenge!

This challenge will help you create positive triggers you can reflect back to when life presents "not fair" moments or someone is not treating you the way you would like to be treated.

The Reflection Challenge was inspired by you, my reader! In writing my book, I really wanted my "Why" to show through, which is inspiring others to live their dream. I struggled to determine what I could do to stay connected with my readers. This is why I created the Refection Challenge. Now after writing the challenge, I see it clearly and know that through it, I, too, will become a better person. I'm excited to take the challenge with you! Thank you for being the catalyst!

The Reflection Challenge is not a onetime exercise, but a regular challenge you can do every month. I see this challenge as a perfect opportunity to have fun and buddy up. Choose a close friend to do the challenge with and keep each other accountable, or join my Reflection Challenge community and share at reflectionchallenge.com.

Let's do the Reflection Challenge together. It's always more fun to share with others the changes you are experiencing in life as you embark on a journey like the Reflection Challenge. Together we can build the Reflection Challenge Community and stay connected!

If you miss a day, don't let that discourage you or stop you from continuing on for the month. Keep moving forward and next month try not to let that same day slip. Remember it takes time to create a habit, just don't give up! If another day's challenge connects with you, feel free to do any day's challenge at any time. Embrace what's speaking to you at that moment. Below is just a guide.

Work on your life, not just in it!

Day 1: It's the first day of the month. Spend at least an hour in silence.

This should be for personal time, not professional time. You can meditate, journal, pray or write. This is your time and the longer the better.

Choose a quiet place and if it lands on a day off, maybe go to the lake or in the woods. Make this time special and look forward to it every month. This is why I made it the first challenge of the month. Let's start out the month right. Silence has taught me how important it is to take time to notice your thoughts and to just let them go.

Day 2: Call a grandparent, parent, sibling, aunt, uncle or someone very close to you.

(Someone you don't call as often as you should.)

The people we are closest to are the ones that we often neglect. Let's change that together. Why do we do this when they are the people we should be giving our best? Because they love us and it's easy to push them aside. Not anymore. Make sure this person is someone that you usually don't call like you should. Your mother or sister?

My mom and sister have a joke. They will call my voicemail and if they hear a new voicemail with today's date, they know I'm still alive. This is because I change my voicemail every day. Funny or sad? You decide. Everyone laughs when my mom and sister tell this story, but I'm not proud of it and am going to change this.

If you were going to die tomorrow who would you call and what would you say? And why are you waiting? Maybe write a letter and read it to them.

Day 3: Pamper Yourself Today.

Another day for you. A date by yourself. You have to make time and pamper yourself.

Get a massage or a pedicure or even better, both!

Take a nap in the middle of the day.

Sh-Sh shopping day? Sorry for my men readers. This one is most likely for the girls. Ok, for the men… Maybe a nice shave at the barber shop or a day on the golf course.

Eat your favorite dessert. Just one day a month is okay.

Take a nice, long, warm bath and read your favorite novel.

Do you need a reason why you should pamper yourself? You shouldn't, but you may find it easier if you can support it with a why. The why is you deserve it! You may have many reasons why you shouldn't but not today. Just do it! Take care of yourself so you can be better for others.

Day 4: Send a handwritten note expressing gratitude.

This can be sent to anyone, close or not close to you. Who has done something kind for you that you can say thank you to? Don't use a stock card but instead stop off at a card shop and pick up a special one just for them. Make it special, make them feel special.

Think how you feel when you get a handwritten note, especially one in the mail. A keepsake you can go back to and that shows someone is thinking about you.

Day 5: Forgive someone that did something wrong to you. The bigger, the better!

Think of someone who has wronged you in the recent or not so recent past, it really doesn't matter. I'm sure you can come up with a list of people if you think about it and have that list ready to choose from for the months ahead. Just do one and save the rest for future months. I'm excited to see the "positive triggers" you will have for your future bad days.

When someone wrongs you it can be hard to get over. You may never be able to reconcile with that person, but only forgiveness will allow you to move on.

Tina Mitchell

Remember when I shared my "Dave Trigger." There are people that we should show more love, acceptance and accountability to.

Day 6:   Now it's the next day, forgive yourself for making a mistake or a wrong choice.

This is "you" time. This is meant to be personal between "you" and "you." Write it down and tear it up or even better, just burn it. I think I'll burn mine.

You can't change the past as it is long gone but forgive yourself so you can move on.

Day 7: Call an old friend to reconnect.

Make sure it's someone that you haven't talked with for at least a year. With Facebook this will be easy. If you don't have their phone number just send them a private message on FB and ask for it. Just say you want to connect, and they will most likely respond.

I live 30 miles from the city I was raised in. I attended elementary, junior high and high school all in the same city. Why do I not make time to connect with my old friends? Why are they old friends and not today's friends? Because I have not made time to connect with them. I will share later in my professional core practice, *Get Connected*, how important it is to connect with the people you need to help your business, but we need to also connect with people in our personal life.

This is something I need to improve. I have been focused for so many years on my professional life, I have neglected my personal life when it comes to connecting.

I teach that life is balanced and this is no different. I'm committed. Are you?

There is always time if you make the time!

Make sure to make this call about the person you are reaching out to, not yourself. Use the FORD conversation (I will share in my professional core practice *Get Connected,*) to get started.

Day 8: Sit with a trusted friend/coach/therapist and pour your heart out.

This doesn't have to take much time. You can just take a few minutes if you want and share how you really feel. It's okay if you feel depressed, not deserving or not confident. Be honest and vulnerable. Get it off your chest so you can move on.

I know I have feelings like this some days. When those feelings are shared, the release is the same as on "Day 5" when you burn your note to yourself. The burden is gone and you can move on.

Sometimes you have to let out the bad so you can make room for the good. This is not the time to complain about someone else. It's time to share that you are not perfect and have days you don't feel confident and just need someone to share it with. Your friends will appreciate your vulnerability.

Day 9: Pay someone, anyone a compliment, a true deep thought-out compliment.

Have you ever had someone pay you a compliment like this? It feels good, doesn't it? Now do this for someone else and see how it feels.

Day 10: Reflect on what your life will look like five years from now.

What is your dream and what does your life look like? Use one of the visualization techniques I shared with you in my personal core practice, *Dream.*

You may already do this every night before you go to bed, but that is your regular routine. This day is extra special. Make it at a special time; slate it between 12-3 p.m., right in the middle of the day. Take 15 to 30 minutes and just dream. Shut your office door or put a "do not disturb" sign outside your cubicle that says, "My time to dream."

Day 11: Unexpectedly do something for a stranger.

I do this every day when I smile at a stranger, let someone over in traffic or give them my perfect parking spot.

This day will be different… Let me think… I got it. I'll go through Starbucks drive through and buy the cars behind me their coffee. Or… I got another one, I'm going to stop off at the grocery store and pick up one yellow rose and give it to the first stranger I see this morning. I guess it will be someone I meet at the cash register. OMG, I'm so excited and I will look forward to this day the most!

These are going to be a few of mine. What will be yours? I can't wait for you to share with me! We can all get ideas from each other.

Day 12: Do something spontaneous. This is another one that is all about you! You and you alone.

(Remember this is spontaneous so don't plan it out)

Do you have a bucket list? If you don't, make one; but make it an easy bucket list of things you can do in a day so it is simple for you to be spontaneous. You want to have your list ready so when you wake up this morning, you just close your eyes and point to the page. Where did your finger land? Okay, this is what you will do.

I think on my list I will have: Go to a theater all by myself and get a big bag of popcorn, cotton candy and a pop! The pop I never do, but it would be spontaneous so I may just do it!

I think I will also have on my list: Stop by the pet store and play with the animals.

I know I will definitely have on my list: Stop by the lake in Kirkland and lay on the grass and jam to my favorite inspirational music.

When crossing the 520 bridge I always see kayakers and say to myself "that would be fun." Why have I never done it? Well, I will!

I might even climb a tree like I did as a child. I have never done this as an adult.

I have so many ideas but I want to save sharing them for when I'm in the moment with you, my readers!

Please share your spontaneous small bucket list with me, so I can be inspired by your ideas, too.

Tina Mitchell

Day 13: Help someone with something.

(Someone close to you, or not. Just help someone!)

This can be big or small. I know if this was Dave's, he would mow someone's yard, but not me. It must be something you enjoy!

You may make a future commitment. Offer to cover a coworkers shift. Give them an IOU card. I have always wanted to just volunteer at a restaurant as a waitress just to experience my younger years, and I know this would build new triggers of memories of my early years. I can easily do this, because I have friends that own restaurants. I just need to do it. Have fun could this be?

Maybe I could show up on the strawberry fields in Puyallup and pick, but give my earnings to one of the working families. This would be considered helping someone.

Offer to babysit a friend's child. Stephanie and Keoki you will love reading this one. Zoe and Claire, are you up for it?

What about offering to help someone move? Okay, this would be another Dave one. I don't know about me. Maybe I could garden for someone.

Day 14: Send someone flowers.

You can do this for anyone you care about or anyone that you haven't made time to get to know, who is a good person. What a way to say, "You are deserving." Sending flowers will make their day and maybe change it all together!

Day 15: We are halfway through the month and look how good it feels so far! Now let's surprise someone with a visit.

I have neighbors that I never just stop by to see. This may be a challenge for me but I guess that's why I named it the "Reflection Challenge." I may also drive to one of my referral partners and just stop in to say, "Hi."

I have friends in other states. What if I just popped in for a visit? Two of them live in Arizona. I could do two with one visit. I'm committed and will do this. Dan and Tami, you will never know when but I'm coming!

Day 16: Let's do something crazy.

I live in Seattle so if it's raining, I'm going running!

Maybe on another day I will go downtown and hold out a sign that says, "Live Your Dream Now."

Or maybe I will just jump into Lake Washington in the winter.

Day 17: Declutter something in your home or office.

If I do this every month I will never have anything in my home or office in disarray. Congratulations if this is the case, you get to take this day off. Before you do, don't forget to check all those junk drawers.

Day 18: Volunteer your time.

I do this on a regular basis and I will say from experience, it's one of the best ones on the list, especially if you volunteer your time at a shelter.

Another good place to volunteer your time is at schools. We all have a unique gift and message that we can share with our children. Your message can change their lives. They are so impressionable at their young ages.

What about a senior community? There are so many seniors that don't have anyone. Volunteer your time to just sit with them. I love to play cards, this would be fun. Canasta anyone? I miss playing Canasta with my grandma.

If you don't have much time this day, just ask anyone you run into that day what you can help them with. Leave it as an open ended question. If they say, "Nothing," move on to the next person, if they say, "Nothing," too, explain what you are doing and that today's challenge is to volunteer your time. I'm sure they will be willing help you and have something you can do for them.

I'm going to add to my charitable time to volunteer at an animal shelter. I just have to be careful with this one, because knowing me, I would want to take an animal home.

Have fun on this day!

Day 19: Work on a bad habit.

Stay on the same bad habit until you have mastered it and then move to another one. You will not quit a bad habit overnight; it will take time and maybe a long time, and that's okay. Just keep working on it, and don't quit or move on until you have nailed this one.

Don't forget, as I mentioned earlier when you are trying to stop a bad habit, focus on the gain not what you are giving up.

I can't wait to hear from you on this challenge.

Day 20: Spend quality time with someone special to you.

Today's the day to set a date with your significant other, your closest friend, or a family member.

Just pick up the phone and schedule them. If we don't intentionally do this, we may find that by the end of the month we have not made time for a date we know we want.

Make a special date with your child. What do they want to do that you have not made time to do with them? You know you will have fun whatever it is, since the time is spent with your child. This is the day to do it. Play a game? Playing dollhouse or with Barbies? What about the ballpark?

Maybe go out on the town or just watch a great movie with your special someone at home. Anything they want to do. Let them decide! Maybe I'll watch a sports game with Dave. If you know me, you know this day is surely not about me. Sports? On the other hand, I will be spending quality time with my husband so I will enjoy the moment.

Day 21: Tell someone what you will do to improve your relationship with them.

After spending quality time with your special person from yesterday, now commit to do something you know they would love you to do.

Maybe you could commit to not take calls during a certain time of the day.

Maybe you can pitch in more. You will know what they want.

Make sure you can follow through with what you are saying you will do. You don't want to commit and then not do it, so it's fine if it is something easy and small. Sometimes the smallest gestures mean the most.

Maybe I will give Dave a back rub. He is the one who always gives me back rubs. Maybe I will do the laundry or unload the dishwasher. Dave always does these too. I know what you are thinking, "What a great husband!" You would be correct.

Day 22: Donate money to a good cause.

There are so many places you can donate money. What is important to you? Think about it and make a donation today.

If finances are tight, think about donating clothes. I'm sure you can find things in your closet that you have not worn in six months. It's time to donate them.

Day 23: Do something that makes you uncomfortable.

Something that many people can relate to is public speaking. Just do it. The benefit of doing something that makes you uncomfortable is that you may just find out you're really good at it.

Are you afraid of heights? You don't have to jump out of a plane but conquer your fear today. Conquer your fears and you will grow into the person you are meant to be.

With this challenge it's important to share it with someone so you have an accountability partner.

Day 24: Spend time in nature.

I love nature. Nature, when you embrace it, is like magic and can transform you. This challenge is a natural way to get to that special place.

I think nature is spiritual and inspires creativity.

Take a hike in the woods.
Take a rowboat or kayak trip.
Garden in your yard.
Camp in your backyard.
Take your dog to the dog park.
Is it snowing? Go play in it!

Day 25: Disconnect from one thing for the day.

No phone, no email, no social media or no TV. Just one thing, that's all.

Day 26: Create something that has nothing to do with work.

Cook a great meal.
Do a craft.

Perhaps share this Reflection Challenge with someone on your list when making a surprise visit (Day 15)

Day 27: Take inventory of the people around you.

Any person that is taking energy from you, reevaluate that relationship.

It's important when becoming the person you want to be, to continue to take inventory of the people you have in your space that are bringing you down.

If you want to be a different person, you may need to change the people who surround you.

Day 28: Express compassion to someone in pain.

Do you spend time on social media? Be intentional today and reach out to someone that needs a friend. If they're talking about a feeling or need, they are asking for help, and you can choose to be there for them. Your kind words can go a long way.

Today you can also pay attention to body language by observing those around you; you can tell if someone needs to get something off their chest. Today's the day to listen.

Day 29: Today don't react negatively to anything or anyone all day.

On this day it's important to make note of the tempting things that would have normally caused a reaction from you. After you do this challenge every month, you will find that you have trained yourself not to react and this day will just become a free day.

Just think how great your life would be if you embraced love, acceptance and accountability.

Day 30: Ask what is really important to someone and then take time to really listen.

Once you take note of what is really important to someone, you can use this information on another reflection challenge day.

Everyone desires to be heard. When listening you validate and acknowledge them. We all want to know we matter and that we are important. All it takes is to truly listen to them.

I think as you do the Reflection Challenge you will realize that you have more free time than you knew. You may recognize the free time that you have is being wasted on things that will not help you grow, like TV or maybe sleeping in? Make your time count by improving yourself and the lives around you.

How excited are you about your life? Are you embracing every second of your day to live your life for you and for others? This is what the Reflection Challenge is all about.

I am excited to be your Reflection Challenge partner, so please share!

I named it the Reflection Challenge because I wanted to help us all create "positive triggers" we can reflect back to when the day is not going so well.

I know it may be hard to do all 30 every month but do your best. Start with your favorite day's challenges and add as you can. Just think if you did make time to do something great everyday how your life would change.

Be intentional and live an intentional life!

Let's change the world together! One day and one challenge at a time!

A must watch movie if you have not have already seen it, is "Pay It Forward" released in 2000. Even if you have seen it, I encourage you to watch it again. It's an unforgettable movie.

What can you do to change the world?

Martin Luther King
1929-1968
"Darkness cannot drive out darkness; only light can do that. Hate cannot drive out hate; only love can do that."

Abraham Lincoln
1809-1865
"I destroy my enemies when I make them my friends."

Dr. Martin Luther King, Jr.
1929-1968
"I have decided to stick to love… Hate is too great a burden to bear."

Nelson Mandela

1918-2013

"Courageous people do not fear forgiving, for the sake of peace."

Mahatma Gandhi

1869-1948

"The best way to find yourself is to lose yourself in the service of others."

Mother Teresa

1910-1997

"I alone cannot change the world, but I can cast a stone across the waters to create many ripples...."

"Let us always meet each other with smile, and the smile is the beginning of love.... We cannot all do great things, but we can do small things with great love."

My husband once asked me who I thought was the most successful person. I said, without thinking, Mother Teresa. I surprised myself with my answer because I thought I would have said Oprah, but my first gut thought was a women that was living a life of purpose. Not to say that being financially successful shouldn't be important to you – it is to me – but what I realized with this question was that financial success is nothing without purposeful success. I live my life striving to be both.

How will you live your life?

Tina Mitchell

CHAPTER 8 - LEARN TO FAIL

"Life is balanced with no exceptions. Every failure has a gain waiting on the other side. Make the decision to look for the gain and not focus on the loss."

- Tina Mitchell

Be willing to fail and success will be yours!

Strength comes from within and is about overcoming the impossible. Say, "Yes, I can." Don't say, "No, I can't."

We have all failed and will continue to do so.

Life will throw you failures and will continue to do so.

The secret is not to give up. Keep trying and push through the failures. It's guaranteed that you will fail if you give up.

Failing is when something doesn't work out and you try again. Failure is when you give up!

Get up every morning ready to conquer the day. Today will be your day if you want it to be. It's up to you.

Don't be fearful of failure. Fear is worrying about something that has not yet happened. Confidence is believing in something that has not yet happened. You have to fail to succeed.

Fear something and run from it or face fear and rise up to it.

I once participated in a self defense class, and you learn how to use your own adrenaline to take your attacker down. The fear you feel in life is the same. You can use that adrenaline to fight back. You will never be stronger than in that moment. What about a mother being able to pick up a car when her child is trapped underneath? This is possible because she used adrenaline to gain strength. If the mother had tried picking up that car the next day and there was no danger, she would not be able to lift it. This is known as hysterical strength, or superhuman strength, and is when extreme strength, beyond what is believed to be normal, can be witnessed.

When people are attacked, why are some able to fight their way out of the situation when others are taken down by their attacker? The reason is because if you don't know how to use your adrenaline, it can't help you. Fear is this way, too. If you don't know how to use your fear to fight, your fear will take you down.

Do you see how powerful fear can be? You can go further than you could have ever imagined because of your fear. Use it!

▸ **You lost a deal.**
If you're in sales, you know what I am talking about. I don't know about you, but I can't think of anyone in any sales position who has not lost a deal. Not only that, but the ones who sell the most have lost the most deals.

▸ **Your plan failed.**
We have all had a plan fail, and if you have not, you are not trying anything out. Remember it's not about "the" plan, it's about "a" plan. Look at the failed plan as a benefit and just think about all you learned from that failure. The great news is there is always another plan. Just keep trying and you will figure it out.

▸ You didn't get the job.

Even though you felt you were the best candidate for the position, you didn't get the job? That's okay. There are other jobs, and maybe that job wasn't right for you anyway. What did you learn, what feedback to improve your skills were you provided that you may never have figured out if not turned down for that job?

▸ You failed on a test.

Have you ever studied really hard for a test? You didn't take any shortcuts but instead read all the reading material and spent hours preparing for it, only to fail? Well, that's okay because think about all that studying and what you learned during the preparation. Don't give up because when you go back the next time, it will be much easier as you are not starting from the beginning, but instead you have all this new knowledge in preparing for the last test. If you fail again, try again.

Keep trying until you pass, and you are guaranteed to succeed. Give up and failure is guaranteed.

▸ You lost the game or competition even though you gave it everything you had.

You can't win every game or competition but you can embrace every loss you experience. This is a good time to reflect on how you got there. You made it, didn't you? What if you never made it at all? There will be other competitions, right?

▸ You experienced a tragedy in life.

This happens to all of us. But you can get through it if you use your hidden strength to pull through it. This strength you will never experience unless you are forced to draw from it because of this tragedy. It's the same as the adrenaline I was just talking about.

What did life throw at you?

Well, I will share what life has thrown my way later in this chapter. I'm just glad I finally understand why and figured life out.

You get to choose if you want to be happy or let life defeat you!

What will you do?

You can look back at a failure and see nothing good came of it, but these are not your trigger points to get through your future failures. You want to look back at the ones that did connect because these will be your inspiration moving forward in life. These too, you will have! Don't miss them!

This is what I was talking about in *Be Alert*. Having "positive triggers" gives you a place to go to, making you feel better instantly. What can be a better trigger, than a failure that turned out to be a blessing that it happened? You will only see these when you are fully watching for them.

Have you ever looked back after a failure or loss and came to the realization that you got through it? What a great feeling it is, a better feeling than when you just easily succeeded.

If you haven't failed, you're not trying hard enough, and failure is all you will have.

Just because you lost, does not make you a loser.

Just because you failed, does not mean you are a failure.

The most successful people have figured out how to turn their failures into successes.

Thomas Edison is quoted as saying, "Our greatest weakness lies in giving up. The most certain way to succeed is always to try just one more time."

Do you know how many times Thomas Edison had to fail to create the lightbulb? 10,000! Can you believe it? He tried 10,000 times before he got it right. Do you have that kind of stamina? Yes, you do, we all do! Just believe in yourself and don't give up!

Remember when you were a child and you tried to learn how to ride a bike? Did you give up after the first fall? No, you got back on your bike and tried again. Even though the next time you knew that the fall was coming and that the fall was going to hurt, you still got back on your bike. You kept doing this over and over again until you finally succeeded. Why do we lose the ability and strength we knew as a child when we get into our adulthood? Live your adult life as you did as a child. Live your life with courage, passion, an endless amount of energy and excitement for life.

Successful people come from all walks of life.

Not all had high IQ's (I don't). Not all attend Ivy League Colleges (I never went to college) or come from wealthy families (you know I did not). Not all of them came from a family that loved and supported them (one out of four, that's all I needed).

Famous Failures

He was rejected from the USA film school 3 times.
Steven Spielberg
Legendary Director Winner of 3 Academy Awards

He was turned down by 27 different publishers.
Dr. Seuss
World famous author

His fiancé died, he failed in business, he suffered a number of nervous breakdowns and was defeated in 8 different elections.
Abraham Lincoln
Sixteenth American President 1861-1865

At age 30, he was left depressed and devastated after being fired from the company he founded.
Steve Jobs
Cofounder, CEO and Chairman of Apple Inc.

His music teacher said, "As a composer, he is hopeless."
Ludwig Van Beethoven
Legendary classical composer

Tina Mitchell

She was demoted from her job as news anchor, because she "wasn't fit for television."

Oprah Winfrey

Famous talk show host

He was fired from a newspaper company because he "lacked imagination" and had "no original ideas."

Walt Disney

Cofounder of the Walt Disney Company and winner of 22 Academy Awards

After being cut from his high school basketball team, he went home, locked himself in his room and cried.

Michael Jordan

World famous basketball player

Rejected by a recording studio, that said: "We don't like their sound. They have no future in show business."

The Beatles

Legendary rock band

He wasn't able to speak until he was 4 and he couldn't read until 7. Parents and teachers worried he might be mentally handicapped and said, "He would never amount to much."

Albert Einstein

Legendary Physicist

His teacher told him he was "Too stupid to learn anything."

Thomas Edison

Inventor of the light bulb

I found these quotes in a video by Jazza Vock on YouTube, but there are so many inspirational people with stories to learn from.

Take control of your life, don't let life control you!

What successful people have in common is that they make their thoughts their realities. The difference seen in successful people is that they only focus on their positive thoughts, not their negative thoughts. This takes practice, commitment, and courage but you can do it!

You haven't failed until you stop trying. When you start over, you are not starting from the beginning, but you are starting from where you left off.

In life and in business… to be successful you need three things…

You must believe in yourself, exercise confidence and commit to hard work!

When I sold Girl Scout cookies, I worked hard, late into the evenings and on weekends.

When I competed with my violin, I practiced two to three hours a day.

When I picked strawberries, I gave up my summers with my friends (and I was a very social child), so this was a big sacrifice.

(Below are successes I will share with you later)

When I worked at Denny's, I pulled back-to-back double shifts.

When I managed the lounge, and had no clientele, I went to the competitors and took them.

When I started in the mortgage industry with no experience and bad in math, I worked long hours to build my skills and didn't listen to the people who told me I couldn't do it.

When I developed my software, I went without sleep for many days. I didn't give up on my dream even though it took over 7 years to reach it.

I did these things because that is what it took to achieve my dreams!

Don't let success go to your head, and just as important don't let failure go to your heart!

Life is balanced – so it is not fair all the time but only some of the time. Do you focus on the not fair or the fair times? What you focus on becomes your reality.

Make what you want out of life or life will make what it wants out of you.

You don't want to miss the sun after a storm, the opportunity after the difficulty or the boom after the recession. It has always been this way!

How do you see life?

Only when you change the way you look at life, will your life change!

Focus on the beauty in life and live a beautiful life, focus on the bad in life and watch your life go downhill. Our thoughts attract more of the same.

I had to learn to fail before I could learn how to succeed in life. I had to learn that everything wasn't fair in life and only I could make the choice on how to deal with it. I had to have tremendous loss before I could see that I still had control of my life.

Remember when I went to Aberdeen, Scotland, and played in the International Festival of Youth Orchestras when I was 12 years old? Well, when I got home from Europe, my life would change and my entire world would collapse. I made the decision to put all my focus on what was not fair and that focus damaged many years of my life. I made the choice to turn down the wrong road. This was the summer after I returned home from Europe, at the height of my young violin career in 1981. It was the summer before I started junior high.

My dad tried taking his life by slitting both of his wrists. After leaving the hospital, he went directly to a psychiatric ward. "What happened to my dad? Where did he go? Why did this happen?" were questions I would ask myself.

When I visited my dad in the psychiatric ward, it was as if he had lost his life but he was still alive. His smile was gone, the sparkle I used to see in his eyes had vanished. What happened to him? What could I do to bring my daddy back? I was scared and felt lost without him. He was still there but at the same time he was gone. I didn't understand why and wondered what I was going to do.

When he did finally come home, he could no longer work because he was a metal plater and needed the use of his hands. The immobility left in his hands made him not hirable. Not to mention, if before he was not motivated to work, he now was in such a bad mental space he went downhill fast. My mom had no choice but to ask my dad to leave and move to California with his sister, where he would remain until his death in 2014. He needed more help than my mom could provide and she now had to get a job to support her two girls.

My heart cried out, "What??? How could my mom do this to my dad?" It was as if she had ripped him away from me. No longer would I be able to feel his arms around me, to protect me. I wondered, "How could she send him away, and worst yet, send him so far away to another state? When would I be able to see him again?"

As it turned out, my dad would not be a part of my life for many years, not until I was an adult. I think the shame was too much for him. Fortunately we were able to reconnect before he died. I wish he could have read my book to see how amazing my life was as young girl when he was a part of it and what an amazing dad he was to me. I know he knew this before he died, but he would have really enjoyed seeing my words in writing and just maybe that would have helped with some of the guilt he felt.

It seemed so unfair to me. Being daddy's little girl, I was devastated. I was so mad at my mom, mad at the world and so sad that my dad was gone. I let this unfairness shape my life for many years to come. Everything I had accomplished in my younger years was as if it never happened. How could one event in life cause me to lose the person I was for as far back as I can remember? What would happen to that little girl that had so much belief in herself, confidence to conquer the world and anything she set her mind to do, and the work ethic to make it happen?

How could one day change everything I was and wanted to be? The answer to this question is, because I let it. I allowed my hurt, pain and anger to take me over and take me down.

I made the decision to leave our little family home in Federal Way just as my dad was forced to do (as I saw it) and move in with my friend. My mom didn't know what to do but let me try to deal with this tragedy the way I insisted. I was a stubborn child. Before this event my stubbornness was positive as I used it to succeed, but now my stubbornness was a disadvantage because I would not listen to anyone. I was going to do what I was going to do. I was old enough to make my own decisions... After all, I was going to be in junior high school. I would live with my friend and her family (any family was better than mine) or just run away. Wow, even today I can't imagine what my mom went through. As I grew up I realized my mom had no other options. She had to make the hard choice to move on without my dad to ensure that the three of us could have a better life.

My teenage years were hard and challenging. I made bad choices, still harnessing the anger I felt from not having my dad in my life. I started hanging out with the wrong crowd and getting into a lot trouble. By the age of 15, I started dating a 20 year old man. Michael Parker became my first husband at 18. I married him, a classic try at young love. I thought I knew it all. My mom dealt with this situation the best way she could. I moved in with him when I was a senior in high school and graduated pregnant.

Our baby girl, Amber Lynn Parker was born on August 29, 1986. Being pregnant changed everything for Mike and me. Before I got pregnant Mike and I were heading down a bad road, and I don't know how far down that road I would have continued if not for Amber. We had something special to build on. A new baby girl was to come into our lives. Her birth was critical to awakening my journey of self-discovery.

Mike got a job remodeling a home in Tacoma, Washington. It was a beautiful place to start our first year with our new baby girl. We lived there, and Mike's services were to act as rent payment.

Everything was so perfect and beautiful. I had my own family now and I could clearly see my future and began to dream again. Those first few months with Amber were some of the most special months of my life. The love I felt as a mother was the best feeling I have ever experienced. I know that all mothers reading my book can understand. The love she gave back to me was the most beautiful thing in my life. I would look into her eyes and see my life as a mother and the amazing daughter I would raise; all the things I would teach her and she would teach me. I knew I would be an amazing mother and could already feel the success of motherhood. I had finally turned to a different page in my book, and felt magical things would now be coming my way.

Yet, it was not meant to be. Life happened again and we lost Amber to SIDS, Sudden Infant Death Syndrome, on December 29, 1986. It was a Tuesday morning at 9 a.m. and Amber was still sleeping. This was late for her as she usually was up much earlier but I let her sleep in, enabling me time to get things done around our home. When I decided to check on her, that's when I found her lifeless body in her crib, a sight I'll never forget and wish I had never seen.

For four short months I was able to experience the magic of motherhood, only to have her abruptly taken away from me. Then just six months after the loss of our child, Mike was arrested for armed robbery and sentenced to seven years in prison. After the loss of Amber, Mike went down fast. My baby girl was gone and so was my childhood sweetheart, the love of my young life. Mike had made a tragic mistake but I still loved him, and he was the only part of Amber I had left.

Why was this happening to me? What did I do to deserve this? What a mean trick life played on me. So much joy was brought into my life, just to have it all taken away. I felt as if I was ready to fall off the edge of life but I had to pull myself out of my deep depression and find the strength to get through this. With all the pain in life you can find strength, strength you never knew you had. I used this strength to fight for my life and for Mike's. I remembered back to the time when my dad tried taking his life and knew I had a choice, only a choice I could make. I could let the unfairness in life take me down or I could fight. I remembered what happened when I lost control of my life before and this time I was not going to let that happen!

What I didn't know in this moment was how both these life experiences would shape my life and change it forever. The loss of Amber was a pain that I have never felt again and hope I never will. But, without this miracle of life and the few months I had with her, would I have ever released myself from the pain I was feeling in life prior to Amber? Without my husband being taken away from me, leaving me all alone in the world, would I had ever found my true inner strength? I don't know.

After Mike was sentenced and taken off to prison, I was determined to make a safe place for him and myself for when he returned home. For the first time since I was a child, my dream was so clear I could feel it, taste it and it was already mine.

Making the long trips to McNeil Island Prison and to Walla Walla State Prison where Mike served his sentence (partially at both prisons), had me dreaming and visualizing again. I would dream during the entire drive about our future life together. I would visualize us grocery shopping, holding hands in the park and laying on the grass discussing our future family plans. This was when I started using my drive time to visualize and, to this day, my car is now my special place as it's the time I spend visualizing. Many of my "aha" moments and moments of inspiration have been created while driving. Would I have ever got to this space without this intense experience? I don't know, but I choose to look at what was gained and not what was lost.

It wasn't meant to be. After Mike returned home four years and seven months after going to prison, there would be no recovery for him. His experience there was too traumatic. For the remaining time of his life here on earth, Mike never escaped his inner demons.

Mike was a good man and had a big heart but was too far gone. Even though he had a safe home to come home to, which I purchased at the age of 21, while he was incarcerated. Even though my dream was so real, it could not save both of us, and our life together was not to be. After eight short months from his return home from prison, I had to divorce him, and move on with my life. Life happened once again, and I could not control it this time either. During the time Mike and I were apart I had grown up and grown back into the person I was when I was a young child. Strong, confident and ready to conquer the world – my world – and Mike no longer fit into it. Once Mike came home, I then realized he had changed. He was doing things that would damage the person I now was. I had to protect that person, the person I always had in me. I was back, and I wasn't going to look back.

I could choose to let life take me down or decide to fight again. I was ready for the fight back then and I am ready to fight today when life hits me.

Now is not the time for you to give up either. You know you can do it, it is your day and it is your life, make it happen! Don't let life take you down!

I would go on to be a successful waitress at Denny's restaurant in Federal Way, moving into a fill-in management position, later to running a hotel lounge at the Holiday Inn in Bellevue, then changing careers from food and beverage to the mortgage industry. Within a few years of starting my career, I became one of the top 200 mortgage professionals in the country. I have developed a mortgage software available to mortgage professionals nationwide and host my own radio show. I have shared my personal and professional core practices in workshops. Who could imagine that now you would be reading my book on my Personal and Professional Core Practices?

If I can do it, you can do it too! Life is unfair but at the same time magical, isn't it? What will you choose to do? How will you address your life challenges? What will you accomplish in your life?

Life is life and will continue to be so. It is balanced, and this means you will continue to have failures but also successes. You will experience losses, not always happiness. Not that all failures and losses will have a gain directly connected to them, but because of balance, there has to be something of equal magnitude to turn to.

Why sit around and hope your luck will change? It's up to you to change your life during unlucky times.

I never wish for a better life, but instead I'm committed to being better at life.

You get to choose!

Tina Mitchell

Why do you face challenges? So you can conquer them. Why does sadness visit you? So you can move towards happiness. Why do you fail? So you can succeed.

Richard Hagerman and Donna Whitson (now Donna Norris) called the FBI and news media when their 9-year-old Amber Hagerman went missing. She was abducted and murdered in Arlington, Texas in 1996. They and their neighbors searched for Amber. Four days after the abduction, a man walking his dog found her body in a storm drainage ditch. Her killer has not been found, and her homicide remains unsolved.

Within days of Amber's death, Donna was "calling for tougher laws governing sex offenders." Amber's parents soon established People Against Sex Offenders (P.A.S.O.) They collected signatures hoping to force the Texas Legislature into passing more stringent laws to protect children. Now we have an AMBER Alert, a child abduction alert system in the United States due to their efforts. AMBER is officially a backronym for America's Missing: Broadcast Emergency Response, but was originally named for Amber Hagerman.

Did life defeat Richard and Donna?

John Walsh's son Adam John Walsh (November 14, 1974 – July 27, 1981) was abducted in a Sears Department store at the Hollywood Mall in Hollywood, Florida, on July 27, 1981. His son was later found raped, murdered and decapitated. John Walsh became an advocate for victims of violent crimes as well as the host of the television program America's Most Wanted.

Did John let life take him down?

Candace Lightner is the American organizer and founding president of Mothers Against Drunk Driving (MADD). On May 3, 1980, her 13-year-old daughter, Cari, was killed by a hit-and-run drunk driver in Fair Oaks, California. When Candace heard the sentence given to her daughter's killer, a repeat offender of driving while intoxicated (DWI), she was outraged and organized Mothers Against Drunk Drivers. The organization name was later changed to Mothers Against Drunk Driving.

Candace wanted to raise public awareness to the serious nature of drunk driving and promote tougher legislation against the crime. She appeared on television shows, spoke before the US Congress, and addressed professional and business groups for many years to change public attitudes, modify judicial behavior, and promote a tough new legislation.

Did Candy put up a fight?

Nick Vujicic Motivational speaker Nick was born with Tetra-Amelia syndrome, meaning he was born with no arms or legs. Discouraged and depressed as a child, he struggled to understand his life's meaning. As a teenager Nick started Life Without Limbs, an organization dedicated to helping those with disabilities discover hope and meaning in life.

Now he is an international speaker, evangelist and daily inspiration to many, including his wife and two children. He won the Australian young citizen award for his bravery in 1990 and in 2005 he was nominated for the Young Australian of the Year Award.

How did Nick view his life? How would you view your life if you were Nick?

Tina Mitchell

Lizzie Velasquez Lizzie is an author, anti-bullying activist and motivational speaker. From the time she was born, she has suffered with a disease that prevents her body from accumulating fat. She has 0% body fat!

As a result, she looks different and has endured bullying remarks most of her life. As a teenager she accidentally discovered a YouTube video where someone featured her as the "world's ugliest woman," a moment that brought cyber-bullying into her life. She chose to allow it to empower her.

Lizzie has turned the sorrow of that moment into good. She completed college, speaks on anti-bullying and teaches compassion in a remarkable, very visual way. Having written multiple books and released her movie, "A Brave Heart: The Lizzie Velasquez Story," Lizzie's influence has worldwide impact, helping others to see the good in themselves.

Did Lizzie embrace her beautiful uniqueness or let people make her believe she was ugly?

These are normal people whose tragedies motivated them to make a change in the world. Big changes!

What will you do if a life tragedy happens to you?

I would like to share a personal tragedy. It's nothing that can compare to the tragedies that Richard Hagerman and Donna Whitson, John Walsh, Candace Lightner, Nick Vujicic, Lizzie Velasquez or I had to get through in my personal life, but is worth sharing as it was a turning point for me in my professional life. One more let down, but it made me into the person I am today. This was when I would develop my personal core practices, *Dream, Be Alert and Learn to Fail,* that I am sharing with you now.

In 2008, I was suddenly faced with the most enormous challenge of my professional and financial life.

The Financial Meltdown

The entire financial market had a meltdown, and I was right in the middle of it, being in the mortgage industry. Not only that, but I was also employed by Countrywide, the mortgage company that took the most heat and blame for the meltdown. My income dropped over 50% within that year, and when the government changed how mortgage compensation plans worked, I lost another 20% of my income. I was dealing with extreme financial stress and was feeling very lost.

I went online for inspiration and motivation and came across the video "Selective Attention Test" from Simons & Chabris followed up by "The Monkey Business Illusion" by Daniel J. Simons. These videos are about perception and changed everything for me. I realized that I could make a choice. It was all about how I chose to view the situation.

Everyone around me was either depressed, angry, or both. These were other mortgage professionals like me. The reality was that we were all coming into an office every day and working. Many others had no job to go to and were relying on other people to hire them. In the mortgage industry we were all entrepreneurs and could make our own success.

After watching these videos I asked myself, "Was anyone buying homes? The answer was, "Yes." As my thoughts went deeper I also

116

came to the conclusion that 70% of the mortgage industry professionals like me had given up and left the business. What did this mean for me and everyone else who were sticking it out? Well, it meant that there were plenty of opportunities for all of us. I was so excited to come to this "aha" moment and I decided to share it with everyone and anyone I could. I shared it with all of my coworkers and then called all of my referral partners and shared my new realization with them too. It gave me a reason to reach out and have some great news to share. I decided in this moment I was going to be excited about the opportunities I had and not focus on the opportunities that were lost.

You see, life is balanced. With all the mortgage professionals exiting the business there was less competition and not only that, there was even better news. The realtors still doing business and clients who were still in the market taking advantage of the huge opportunity to get a home at a discounted price, they needed me more than ever. The industry had changed forever and hopefully for the financial stability of our country will always remain different. To be a mortgage professional, it now took knowledge, experience, hard work, heart and passion to survive. I had everything I needed to be successful.

Can you see the difference between misfortune and opportunity? Can you have one without the other? Isn't the bigger the misfortune the bigger the opportunity? This realization was exciting to have uncovered. It is not always easy, but it's comforting for me to know this. To know that everything in life is balanced, I was better knowing that I would get to make the decision.

I could see the market as an opportunity or a challenge. I made the decision to move forward and turn anything that felt like a challenge into an opportunity.

What I didn't realize at that very moment was what this experience would really do for me.

Driving home that night, thinking to myself as I always do, I realized that everything had an "opposite" or a "preference" or we had a "choice." This realization is now one of my personal core practices and you are currently reading in this chapter, "Learn To Fail." I realized that life is balanced, and I learned to look at loss as an opportunity, but also learned how to accept failure and use it to succeed.

On my drive home that night I stopped at a red light and then thought about the green light, followed by the thought of the road that went up and the road that went down, the over pass and the under pass. For weeks after, I did an exercise and wrote down everything I saw or thought of and asked, "Is there an..." "opposite" or a "preference" or a "choice" and yes, it fell into one of these categories. You try and you, too, will be amazed!

Below are just a very few I started with...

- Sweet or sour?
- Short or tall?
- Hot or cold?
- Bad or good?
- Happy or sad?
- Pleasure or pain?
- Mean or nice?
- Love or hate?

Do you see???
What goes up must come down!
What falls must rise.

Tina Mitchell

Pros and Cons, Do's and Don'ts.

I know it sounds crazy, but to this day I still have the book where I wrote down this exercise. I have pages and pages of words as I continued the exercise for weeks. My team and husband even joined in on the exercise as they saw how much fun I was having. Each coming up with new words to add to my list.

This was the place and this was the time. At this moment life suddenly became a game; a game I would play with myself and today continue to do so. The more I practiced, the better I got. I started to get excited about the day's challenges because I could see how I could turn each challenge into an opportunity. I choose to play my game to win, and see every loss as an opportunity! Every failure I will accept and use as a stepping stone to succeed! Every tragedy I will embrace the strength it will give me to fight on. I made the decision to be powerful and not powerless.

This knowledge would continue to help me as the mortgage industry continually changed and became more challenging. With all the government changes, it kept getting harder to do what I did, and every day a new challenge would present itself. When I wanted to give up and quit I would change my tune. I told myself "if I was feeling like quitting, it was guaranteed that one of my competitors was doing the same." The difference was they were quitting. This meant more opportunity for me if I could just stick it out, and that's exactly what I did.

It was so freeing to know that I was in control of my life. My life was what I made of it.

When taking the long drives to Walla Walla state prison to visit my husband after pulling double shifts at Denny's restaurant, it was not the smartest thing to do. Driving and no sleep are not a good combination. Because of this bad choice I made, I had a few car accidents in my younger years. Through the years I had constant back and neck pain due to my car accidents. When the pain would come, I would focus on the pain and it would get worse and sometimes pretty unbearable. Once embracing and appreciating that everything was balanced, I thought if I could accept failures in life but not put my focus on those failures, it would make things better. Maybe this would work with my back and neck pain. When I felt the pain coming on, I would accept the pain was there then tell the pain to go away. It was as if I was pushing the pain right out of my body. Pretty powerful, isn't it?

How wonderful life really is… and how instructive. Without pain, how can we appreciate what pleasure feels like? Without hate, how can we experience the feeling of love? If there was no failure, how could we know how success really felt? What if you had to eat your favorite food forever? Would it be your favorite anymore?

Life is balanced! Life is a choice! Life is your preference!

Reflecting back on my life I realized missed opportunities, but I'm watching for them now. Just as I am writing my story, in this moment, I have come to a new realization. If it were not for my tragedies in life, I could not be sharing them with you in my book. Just maybe, I can help you come to this realization too! The future is mine, and it's yours too!

This would be the year of the financial meltdown, a year where I would intentionally focus on personal growth and would have many more "aha" moments that have made me the person I am today. I continue and always will continue to work on myself, to continue to grow and learn. Without the financial meltdown, I might have never come to this

Tina Mitchell

realization. My personal core practices may have never been realized if it were not for this life challenge.

I now appreciate the saying, "With age comes wisdom." I also believe that with wisdom comes freedom. The freedom to live life and to appreciate all that life throws at you.

None of us want life to hit us hard and knock us down, but when it does, what will you do? All you have to do is, get up!

What will life throw at you? The more important question is, what will you do about it?

I decided to say, "Yes" to my life. Instead of taking the easy road and saying, "No, I can't get through this." I said, "Yes, I will get through this."

Tina Mitchell

CHAPTER 9 - TAKE RISKS

You have to be willing to take risks. Push yourself out of your comfort zone.

Sometimes you have to believe in the impossible. Decide to make the impossible the possible and take a risk!

Be cautious and live a cautious life. Be willing to take risks and live the life you were meant to live. How can you learn to do something if you don't just jump in and just try!

Today, right now, we all have a problem. Problems are a part of life but they don't have to be your life. Be excited to focus on the solution, learn from the problem and make the decision to make it better. Use your problem to motivate you to take the risk needed to correct it. Push through it and don't allow your problem to take your prize.

Take responsibility for your life. You are in control. If you don't like where you are at, change it. Dig deep for your passion, as your passion will give you the power to fight for what you want out of life!

You are powerful! Use that power to win, don't let your power take you down!

The difficult part is not winning, the difficult part is believing you can! Trying to be right shows weakness, but allowing yourself to be wrong shows strength and will provide the drive needed to take risks.

Once you figure out that you are your own competitor, you will be able to do anything! Don't worry about what anyone else is doing. Stay focused on you and your success, because this is what you can control. If you are focused on someone else, you will lose control and the ability to reach your goal.

Your life is your game and you get to choose if you are playing to win or lose. You are in competition with only yourself and no one else!

Have you ever said someone else is one up on you? You are only one up on yourself. It's you against you.

The harder you fall, the stronger a person you will be when overcoming your failures.

If you do what is easy, your life will be hard. If you do what is difficult and you do it repeatedly, your life will become easy. Take the hard road and live an easy life. Take the easy road and a hard life you will live.

- It's hard to try something you have never done before.
- It's hard to work late when you are tired.
- It's hard to take risks when you already have security.

Now think how hard life will be if you don't do it. Just go for it!

Keep trying again and again until you make it happen!

Only if you take a risk can you see if you can do it!

In my adult life I have taken many risks when it came to my career.

Tina Mitchell

I worked as a janitor for Fred Meyer stores because I needed a job where I could work the graveyard shift, so I could make the long drive to see my husband Mike during the days when he was incarcerated. I worked hard to get promoted to Janitorial Manager and was doing well for my age financially. I knew that this career would not be ideal once Mike was released because he would be working days and I would be working graveyard. I had to come up with a different career path that would allow me to move to a day shift position once he was released from prison.

I thought a waitress at Denny's would be perfect, since it was open 24 hours a day. I determined I could continue to work graveyard until Mike came home so I could visit him during visiting hours in the day and, because with the seniority I would then have, I could move to a day shift once we were together again. I really wanted the job but had no waitress experience and my husband was incarcerated. I was also concerned about the pay because the hourly rate was minimum wage and I would have to depend on my tips to make the money I needed to pay my bills. I could have talked myself out of even trying, but I didn't. I had come up with a plan, a perfect plan. I went in, interviewed for the job and got it. Only a couple of years later, I was asked to be an assistant manager fill-in. I was on my way to managerial training where I could someday run my own store. I made more money as a waitress than I did as a Janitorial Manager at Fred Meyer, and bought my first home while waitressing.

I had just turned 21 and wanted something more. My new dream was hotel management! Should I give up all that I had worked for at Denny's? Should I give up the dream of having my own store someday? "Why not? I can do this!" I told myself.

I had no college education and no hotel experience, so how would this work? I didn't ask these questions. I just made the jump to the Holiday

Inn Lounge in Bellevue, going from a 15 minute commute to an hour commute. I thought I made it into the hotel industry. It was not hotel management, but lounge manager was a start. I went from Denny's where I had regular well-tipping clients. I left just as I was on my way to management training. I had worked so hard to get there and risked giving it all up not even knowing if I could be successful taking a management position in a lounge with no business. No business meant, no tips! But someday I would work my way into hotel management. That was my new dream!

Starting with no clientele, I had to go out and get them. I closed the lounge down for a couple weeks with my business cards in hand and found out where my ideal clients were hanging out for lunch and cocktails, and encouraged them to come see me. I built my clientele with mainly retired men coming in for lunch and business people joining me for happy hour. Business was booming. The lunch hours were packed with regulars and crowded as well during happy hour. My regulars came in for great conversation and it felt like the Cheers Bar from the popular sitcom.

The lounge was doing more business than ever before. I soon started using my space in the lounge during closed hours (early morning) to have breakfast networking meetings to make my department more profitable, even though it added three hours to my already long day. I developed specialty events in the evenings, adding even more hours. Some days I would be at the lounge from open to close, coordinating Broadway shows, Jazz Nights and many more evening events. I would do anything it took to bring in extra income for my department. After 7 fantastic years, the owners sold the hotel to a big chain. The new owners came in and cut the salaries of the department heads and would no longer pay us a percentage of our department's profits. This was devastating to me financially.

Tina Mitchell

It was shocking when I went to interview with other hotels and realized the Dupar's (previous owners of the hotel) really took care of their people financially. They compensated us very well and I would not have this same opportunity with the big chains. I realized the food and beverage industry and my original dream of hotel management would not provide the income potential I desired. This was another time when I could have looked at this as a failure and unfair. I had put all those years into my career, only to have the owners sell and be left out in the cold, so to speak. I didn't wallow in bitterness, but instead realized I needed to make a change. I took the risk needed to leave an industry where my confidence was at a high level to start something new that was intimidating and I knew nothing about.

I was going to be an entrepreneur. This way I would be in control of my success and my financial future. But what would this be? What would I do next? Why not the mortgage industry? Some of the networking breakfasts I had in the lounge gave me the opportunity to meet mortgage professionals. After talking with them I thought this might be a good career path for me to venture into next. I was able to buy my own home and now I could help other people reach their dream of home ownership as well. My math skills were not good, and I had no training, but I knew I could do it!

I interviewed with Wells Fargo but they turned me down. They said I needed two years of experience and to let someone else hire me first. I kept knocking on mortgage companies' doors and was not hired, but would not give up. I finally knocked on John Fairchild's door, the owner of Phoenix Mortgage, and he gave me a chance. "You will not regret it," I said. He hired me, and did not regret it as I excelled during my employment with him, once again reaching new income heights.

When I started in the mortgage industry I decided to go door to door as I did when I was a child selling Girl Scout cookies, but this time was different. I was knocking on real estate company doors. I smiled and had my script prepared but this was the real world, the adult world. I was all grown up and in a grown up profession but with no experience in a very demanding industry where experience was required. With all the "No thank you, I'm already working with an experienced mortgage professional" responses, there were many days when I would tell myself, "I can't do it. I'm not smart enough." I had to quickly change my self-talk if I was going to survive and thrive in the mortgage industry. That's just what I did!

I asked myself, "Why can't I do it? If someone else can, I can too." I decided to stay positive, focus and to work hard on my craft. I would often think of the other challenges I had to overcome and how I succeeded. If I could excel in those, why could I not excel in the mortgage industry too? Remember when I said to reflect on the real moments of success and how this would help you in your future challenges to overcome them as well?

In my first year in the mortgage industry, I earned more than any year at the Holiday Inn. I was then recruited over to Wells Fargo! I know. Can you believe it? The company that I first interviewed with and turned me down, telling me I needed two years experience before they would consider me for employment, was now recruiting me just a year later. I took the position because they offered me a big condo project that I could not turn down. In my second year at Wells Fargo I was the first one in my region to make the Presidents Club, representing the top 50 originators in the entire company. Just a few years into my career, I was named in the top 200 mortgage professionals in the nation in Mortgage Originator Magazine. I had made it! I was a successful entrepreneur.

I talked myself into being successful instead of talking myself out of success!

Tina Mitchell

If you are in sales, a necessary movie to watch is, "Door to Door," a 2002 film inspired by Bill Porter, a door-to-door salesman with cerebral palsy. The film was nominated for and won six Emmy Awards and a Peabody Award.

Porter was unable to gain employment due to his cerebral palsy, but refused to go on disability. Somehow he eventually convinced Watkins Incorporated to give him a door-to-door salesman job. He sold products on a route in the Portland area and eventually became the top seller for the company. Despite the pain of his medical condition, he would walk eight to ten miles a day to support himself. Porter continued to work as a salesman until the age of 69. This is a movie about failing over and over again but not giving up. It also had a special meaning to me because of the emotional support his mom gave him which helped him to succeed in a way that no one could have ever imagined. The same support that my mom gave me.

After watching this movie, you will see that if Bill Porter can do it, you too can!

While still doing mortgages, I also wanted to develop a mortgage software. I had created a massive excel worksheet that made my job much easier when educating my clients on their different loan options. "How do you even create a software?" I asked myself. Well, one of the many mortgage professionals using my worksheet sent his client to me who was a software developer.

His name is Todd Elston and he proposed that we start a company together. If he could be a 50% owner he would take my excel worksheet and develop a web based application version of it at no charge. Five years later after many long hours of work, the owner of

Pinnacle Capital Mortgage (now Finance of America) Robert Boliard approached us and offered us $250,000 for 15% share of our company. The product was unfinished and not on the market yet with no sales, but he believed in us, saw the company's potential and wanted to help. Now Mortgage Triangle Software is available for mortgage professionals around the country and the $250,000 was later gifted to us with 100% of the company being issued back to Todd and me. I know crazy, right? Miracles can happen when you have a dream and are willing to work hard to make that dream become a reality!

This is an example of dreaming with the end in sight and not getting stuck in the how or the middle of the process. I could have had so many questions and concerns. Starting a software company? How could I ever make this happen? All the legal and tax stuff, or the knowledge required to start a company when I had no idea where to even start. Who would help me? Where would the money come from? How could I do this on my own? I never asked these questions, I just shot for my dream!

Todd and I both dedicated years of long hours designing and developing our software while at the same time I continued to work long hours producing at a high level in my mortgage business. The end result? My dream manifested itself.

Dream with the end in sight, be willing to work hard, and things will line up for you as they did for me.

What is next? I don't know, but I do know one thing. It will be with passion and commitment to make a difference in the world, in my own unique way, one person at a time, one day at a time, and one dream at a time.

Tina Mitchell

If you get out of your comfort zone and just go for it, magical things will happen!

If you don't reach your true potential, you will miss out on the gift you have to share. You have something special to offer the world. Don't waste it!

You will regret what you don't try, not what you fail at trying!

Live your dream now. We all have one!

This is the end of my personal core practices; *Dream, Be Alert & Learn to Fail*. Now I would like to share with you my professional core practices; *One-time Your Business, Embrace Your Strengths & Get Connected*.

Personal and professional successes go hand-in-hand. For me I could not have one without the other.

CHAPTER 10 - ONE-TIME YOUR BUSINESS

"Take control of your business or your business will control you."
- Tina Mitchell

When you have control of your business you can then have control of your life, and that's when magical things will happen for you.

To "one-time" your business is a mindset and a commitment to implementing small "one-timing" activities so that system, processes and communications with your clients are at the highest level possible.

The benefit to you is that you are working less, while at the same time earning more money and having more time to enjoy life.

Isn't that what life is all about?

What you will realize after embracing my "one-time your business" philosophy is that the majority of the stress you feel in your business results from the same issues coming up time and time again. To eliminate this stress just pay attention to the questions, requests, objections and mistakes that come into your office. After tracking them, you will see they are the same ones that come up repeatedly. Why not "one-time" them?

As a business professional myself, I have learned how to "one-time" my business and build a business that is efficient, consistent and replicable.

When you "one-time" your business you will have the time to embrace what you want in your business and what you want out of life.

This benefit, I too, have experienced. "One-timing" my business has provided me the time to be a leader in the mortgage industry, develop a mortgage software, operate as owner of Mortgage Triangle Software, become a radio personality and host of The Money Hour on 1150 AM KKNW, as well as being a speaker, coach and now an author.

More importantly, it has allowed me the time to have a successful family life and to live my purpose; to inspire others to dream. It has provided me the time to share my message with homeless shelters in the Seattle area, including The House of Hope, The Hoff Foundation, and Mary's Place.

I am currently seeking out schools in my local community to share my book with our children. I want to share my childhood with them and the life lessons gained. Perhaps other children can reach their true potential at an earlier age than I have.

Have you ever said, "If I only had the time, I would..."
- ▸ be a better spouse.
- ▸ spend more time with my children.
- ▸ give back to my community.
- ▸ travel the world.

You will be amazed how much time you really have when you "one-time" your business. Listed below are two books that were game changers for me and became the inspiration behind my "one-time your business" philosophy.

<u>Who Moved My Cheese</u> by Spencer Johnson taught me why it's important to adapt to change. The cheese symbol used in the book is a metaphor for what we want in life. The message is that we can learn how to anticipate change, be excited to change and be ready to change over and over again. When you develop a mindset to "one-time your business," you will see that your business will constantly change. Your business can't improve and grow without change!

Everything changes in life. What if you were still rocking that same hair style as you had in the 80's. Or what would your business look like if you had not adapted and changed with technology? It would be non-existent. To survive in business and life, you must be willing to change! What would my mortgage practice look like if I had not been willing to change with the economy?

Darren Hardy has also been a true inspiration for me. I highly encourage you get his book, <u>The Compound Effect</u>. This book is about the principle of reaping huge rewards from a series of small, smart changes.

After hearing Darren speak for the first time back in 2011, everything made sense to me. The power of the compound effect was something I embraced for years but didn't realize I was doing it. I now am intentional in how I approach everything in my life, personally and professionally. Take one small step at a time, and another small step, and another, experiencing the compound effect.

Get a little better every day at your craft. Focus on the end in mind and do not dwell on everything it's going to take to get there. If you spend too much time in the "how," it will deter you from working in the "now." Work on today's task and move forward, one step at a time.

Make small changes and they will have a compound effect. The big changes are not attainable or sustainable most of the time, but the small changes are reachable and manageable. The compound effect can work for you or against you.

Consider the candy jar at the receptionists desk. It's ok to just take one piece of candy when you walk by, isn't it? The problem if you do, is that you have given yourself permission to take one piece of candy every time you walk past that desk. This action will have a compound effect. If you don't take that piece of candy, the compound effect will be much different.

Is the compound effect working for you or against you? We all know crash diets don't work. Why is that? Because they are not sustainable.

Start small and work up to it. Put your tennis shoes by the front door and walk past them every day for a week. Don't put them on, just walk past them. Next week, put them on and walk a small distance. Do that every day for a week. And then the week after that, get into your car after your walk and drive to the gym. Don't go in, just drive by and look at the gym as you drive by it. Do that for a week. And finally, the last week, go into the gym. Can you see how the small changes you make work up to the big changes, so they become sustainable and you will experience a compound effect? You remember the story about the Chinese Bamboo Tree, don't you?

It's important during this process that if you miss a day, you start over from the beginning. If you don't start over, after losing the momentum, your progress most likely will not be sustainable. You have to create a habit to see the compound effect. You do this by taking a small step, then another and another after that, until you have reached your goal. The compound effect works in your personal and professional life!

Tina Mitchell

Do you want to remain on the hamster wheel? If not, work smarter, not harder!

Are you part of the rat race? If so, do things differently than the majority!

If you're spinning your wheels in business, step back and broaden your horizon.

A rule of thumb states that 80% of outcomes can be attributed to 20% of the causes for a given event. This is know as the Pareto Principle.

- ▸ 80% of your time is spent in 20% of your home.
- ▸ 80% of your time is spent with 20% of your friends.
- ▸ 80% of your drive is to get to 20% of your locations.
- ▸ 80% of your groceries are found in 20% of the store.
- ▸ 20% of the your clothes are worn 80% of the time.
- ▸ 20% of your stories are told 80% of the time.

Pretty crazy, right?

What about your business?

You know the statistics... 80% of sales are made by 20% of the sales team.

Are you a part of the majority of minority?

Then, you have the one percentile. The best of the best. Do you want to be in the one percentile?

"One-time Your Business" and spend 80% of your time being proactive instead of reactive.

Term Definitions

I would like to share some *"One-time Your Business"* terms I will use throughout this professional core practice.

"In Your Business" - Working "in your business," is when you are doing the daily activities you must do to keep your business running.

"On Your Business" - Working "on your business" instead of "in your business" as you do day in and day out. This is when you are creating and developing new ideas to implement into your business model.

"On-time" - The time you block out on your calendar to work "on your business."

"Off-time" - Your free time and days off.

"One Off" - A question, request, objection or mistake that is "one off" and most likely will not come up again. You will have very few "one offs." Most questions, requests, objections and mistakes will be the same and come up repeatedly. This is where you will have the opportunity to "one-time" them.

"One & Done" - Something you develop into your business model to ensure that you do not have to do this task a second time but instead it is a "one & done." This is what you will experience when you "one-time" your business!

Tina Mitchell

"One-Timing" Exercise

A turning point in my business was an exercise that one of my first coaches had me do back in 1999. I was asked to write down every call and email that came into my office. He then asked me to fax it over to him at the end of the day for accountability purposes. I could not see what benefit this would have and thought it would take up time that I did not have. I couldn't believe I just hired someone that was giving me an exercise that would take more time out of my day. Time I didn't have enough of to get done what was needed. If I had not signed a contract, I would have quit the program, and this would have been a big loss for me and my business. What I didn't realize at the time is that this one exercise would completely change how I looked at everything in my business.

I soon realized why he had me do this exercise. The time I thought I didn't have was being wasted, and I was not running an efficient business. This would all change because of this one exercise!

The calls and emails into my office were the same questions and requests coming in over and over again. They were the same objections and issues I needed to address because of the mistakes I repeatedly continued to make. This was a great exercise because it developed a mindset and a commitment to "one-time" my business.

To this day every call and email into my office causes me to wonder how I can "one-time" it. I ask myself, "Is there something I can develop into my business model to ensure I don't have to do this activity a second time, but instead consider it "one & done"?

This is the most powerful exercise to get into the habit of doing. You may have heard it takes 21 days to create a habit, but studies from the University College of London showed it takes an average of 66 days to create a habit. It can take months to start seeing results so don't give up. You too will experience the "one-timing" magic.

Write down every call coming into your office and during your "on-time," one-time it! Also, when responding to emails or texts, ask yourself, "can you one-time them?" If you are having a difficult time with this exercise just go back to your deleted and sent emails and texts. You will be amazed at the "one-timing" opportunities you will find.

Be committed to the "one-timing" exercise.

Do you agree this could be helpful in your business?

"One-timing" Exercise Example

When tracking calls and emails coming into my office, I noticed most of them were not "one offs" but instead the same questions and requests being asked by multiple clients. This is a perfect opportunity to "one-time" your business.

For example, I regularly had clients asking how much their mortgage payment would increase with an additional $10,000 in purchase price. Another common question was how much their mortgage payment would adjust based on a .25% movement in interest rates.

This is a simple calculation I now share upfront so my clients don't have to ask. It's right in my presentation. This is "one-timing!"

Tina Mitchell

"One-timing" was the step that started me on my journey with my excel spreadsheet that is now Mortgage Triangle Software. This is a great example of the result you can experience when "one-timing your business," and as Darren Hardy says, "the compound effect." Make small changes in your business and experience huge results.

Almost everything we do in our business can be "one-timed." Your phone should ring for three reasons; a client is returning your call because you have requested them to do so, a client is calling to say thank you for the amazing service you have provided, or a client is calling to introduce you to new client.

If a client calls for any other reason, write it down and during your monthly "on-time," "one-time" it. I will share later what your monthly "on-time" is.

You may receive personal calls during your business hours and if you do, you will want to one-time them too. Coach your family and friends to respect your business time and ask them to call during your "off-time." Let them know you are committed to being better at that relationship and to do so, you need to be as efficient as possible at work, so you can give 100% to that relationship during your personal time with them. After you share the reason, they will see the benefit and respect your business hours. Can you see how powerful this is?

Take control of your business, and have control of your life! Be better in business, and the best "you" for your relationships!

Quality is better than quantity when it comes to phone calls.

If you're not "one-timing your business," you're doing the same tasks multiple times. Why not "one-time" your system, processes and communications with clients so you're not duplicating your efforts and wasting your time?

This makes sense, doesn't it?

Steps to One-time Your Business

Observe:

Watch others who are at a higher level than you, see what they are doing, and make it your own. Why reinvent the wheel?

When I started in the mortgage industry, I had no idea where to start or what to do. I reached out to the top producers in my company and asked what they were doing. I took note of what resonated with me and then made it my own.

Attend workshops and read books. I think it's good to attend a minimum of one workshop a quarter and read or listen to one audio book each month.

Remember when I left Denny's to go to Holiday Inn how my commute changed from 15 minutes to one hour? Many people complain about their commute, but I took full advantage of it. I decided to maximize my drive and the opportunity to learn during this time. This decision became one of my biggest advantages because I learned more during these years than I had up to this date. I didn't go to college but feel I learned more than if I had. I was able to choose exactly what I wanted to learn. I learned about leadership, team building, how to develop my skills and gain clientele. I got motivated and inspired on my drive!

Tina Mitchell

After moving to the Eastside I went from an hour commute back to a 15 minute commute again and I missed my drive as it was my forced time to learn.

I had to make the intentional decision to not sleep in longer with my now shorter commute, but to instead get into the office earlier. I used this time to continue my learning since I no longer had the commute. I don't know how I could have ever accomplished what I have without this intentional desire to learn and continue to grow, by listening to others through books of education, motivation and inspiration.

You don't have to be brilliant and come up with your own ideas. You just have to be smart enough to observe others.

Everything we learn in life comes from someone; parents, teachers, coaches, mentors or colleagues. The key is to embrace, adopt and make it your own.

You don't have to be a master creator but you do need to be a master implementer.

Did you know you can get all the education you desire online? Do you want to learn from Harvard, Stanford or maybe MIT? Many universities have listed course materials and even some lecture videos online. You don't get the labs or the degree but you get to choose classes based on what interests you. I wasn't focused on a grade, but I focused on the knowledge I would take away from the continued education.

It's also important to observe yourself and your business to see where changes are needed and than be willing to make those changes.

Listen:

Response from your clients and referral partners is one of the best ways to "one-time" your business. Carefully listen to the feedback you receive. Really listen. The feedback will steer you in the direction of change, the change you need to get better at your craft.

Act:

The most important step is to act. Implement and put into action everything you gathered while observing and listening. The best way to implement new ideas into your business is to schedule "on-time."

"On-time" is where you are working "on your business" instead of "in your business," like you do day in and day out. You want to have "on-time" once a month where you shut your door, and take no calls, no emails or interruptions. Just work "on your business."

You'll be amazed at what you can accomplish when you have blocked on your calendar "on-time" just one day a month. It is important that your "on-time" is during normal business hours. If you schedule your "on-time" during your "off-time" (personal time), there are too many excuses you may come up with to interrupt this time.

You may ask if once a month is enough? I would ask you when was the last time you completely shut your business down for an entire day? I mean really shut it down, to only work "on your business" and not "in your business," with no phone calls, no emails, or interruptions.

Yes, once a month is enough.

Tina Mitchell

By the way, you can have "on-time" more than just one day a month if you choose. Your creative juices may be flowing and you may want to take advantage of this. You can do extra work "on your business" as much as you want during your "off-time" (personal time). There have been many long nights with no sleep and long weekends that I have not left the house but instead sat behind my desk creating and evolving my new ideas. Embracing my motivation and inspiration to finish and complete a project has enabled me to implement many new things into my business model. If I didn't have "on-time" during my "off-time," I don't know how many years it would have taken me to write my book, but with the desire to finish it and giving up my personal time, I published it in less than a year.

During normal business hours you must stay focused on the tasks that are necessary to keep your business running. Only during your once a month "on-time" will it be during normal business hours.

Just never cancel this time you have scheduled with yourself as it is critically important to your business. You need to improve your business and the continued growth you need for your business is dependent on this scheduled time.

When you first start doing "on-time," you will want to start out small and more frequently and work up to the once a month, all day. Start out with one hour a day for a few months, then move it to one day a week for an hour for a few more months, and then move into an entire day, once a month. This will allow you to create the habit of doing "on-time."

You must work "on your business" not just "in your business."

"On-time" will change your business! Without it, your business will never reach the levels you want it to.

What do you do during your "on-time?"

Review, Prioritize and Implement

From your "one-timing" exercise, review the list of calls and emails that came into your office. Track questions from your presentation, the objections that came up and mistakes that happened over the month. You will want to "one-time" them!

List as Level 1, 2, or 3

Level 1: The easiest to implement… This would take no effort but just the commitment to making a change. Maybe changing your voice mail every day or committing to time blocking your schedule.

You never want to commit to more than one, level one at a time. Changing your habits takes work. Master one and move to another. Set yourself up for success not failure. Remember it takes time to change your habit and even longer to start seeing results. So give it time!

Level 2: These should not take too much time to implement and are not difficult. Maybe writing email templates, creating forms, scripts, checklists or solving a mistake that came up. Complete as many level 2s as you can during your "on time." This way you will leave the day with a lot accomplished. I will talk about all of these in more detail later.

Level 3: These are the most difficult and take the most time to implement. They are things like creating a website, planning a client event, writing a business plan or maybe implementing a Customer

Tina Mitchell

Relationship Management system (CRM) into your business. You never want to work on more than one level 3 at a time.

Level 3s are what I call "Game Changers." You really need to work on one "Game Changer" at a time or they will suck you down... "Game Changers" are just that... They will have a huge impact on your business and if worked on in an efficient way will be a game changer in your business.

The key here is to list what I call "Needle Movers." Needle movers are the tasks needed to do to make your "Game Changers" come alive. Make your long list of "Needle Movers" but you must only work on one "Needle Mover" at a time. Implement it and then, only then move onto the next "Needle Mover." If you notice you are never adding any substantial ideas to your business, this is because you are not "one-timing" your "Game Changers" and "Needle Movers."

It's important to know that level 3s may be a work in progress. You may get the basic information needed for your website to be up and running. Use what you have and move over to something else if you would like. Sometimes you will get bored or want to use what you have created so far. It's okay to do this and move on to something else.

Perhaps you are implementing a CRM and decide you want to go back to the website at a later date to revisit it. You just don't want to be working on both at the same time.

If I had stayed on my software until it was finished, I still wouldn't be using it, no one else would be benefiting from it either, and I would have never implemented any other level 3s. They may never be done. I will continually be improving and having new functions built into my mortgage software.

These are the steps to enable you to implement and complete!

Remember that during your "on-time" you cannot take calls, return emails or allow for any interruptions. I would put your phone on do not disturb, shut your email down so you don't hear the alerts and definitely close your office door.

At first this will most likely stress you out because you are not used to shutting down your business for a day. Please remember the benefits and remember the risks if you don't.

You attend all day workshops so why can't you shut your business down for a day just once a month? This will have an even bigger impact than a workshop because you are working on your own business, specific to your business needs.

Yes, your business will survive when you shut it down for just one day a month. The real question is: how will your business survive and thrive if you don't?

Do you want to see change in your business? You need three things…

Decision, Will and **Commitment**. Make the decision to change, the will to do it and the commitment to follow through. Your business will be different and you will never look back to your old ways! "On-time" is important!

"On-Time" Makes a Difference

What I see in my industry when people have not blocked on their calendar "on-time" is one of three things…

Tina Mitchell

- They start new projects but never finish them.
- They try implementing new projects during normal business hours and their production goes down.
- They never start new projects at all.

With any of these outcomes is the feeling of defeat and where I believe stress can begin in your business.

Do you see this happen in your industry?

Remember, it's important not to implement or make changes to your business while working "in your business" because this is the time you need to do all the daily activities that keep your business running. Save working on and improving your business for your scheduled "on-time."

This is very important to be successful at "one-timing your business."

Eliminating Objections

Take control of your objections and eliminate them.

I always hear people talk about overcoming objections. Why not eliminate them all together?

Objections do not exist if you eliminate them before they ever come up. The objections your clients have are not "one off" objections, but instead they are the same objections most other clients will have as well.

Learn what the common objections are, address them upfront before they come up, and provide a response that will eliminate them.

Usually in any business you will not see more than ten, making it totally manageable to eliminate them by addressing them upfront.

By eliminating objections instead of overcoming them, they never exist. You will eliminate any doubt your client may have of working with you and will have a higher closing ratio.

The only time eliminating objections upfront will not work is when you are making cold sales calls to get an appointment with someone that doesn't know you.

It is natural for the person on the other end of the line to say, "No" because their subconscious is telling them to say this. Why would they say, "Yes"? They don't even know you!

Be prepared before you pick up the phone and make the call. First you have to make them feel good as soon as they pick up the phone.

"Hi, my name is Tina Mitchell and I am with Absolute Mortgage. The reason for my call is because I have made a decision for my business to align myself with the best in the industry. This is why I am calling you. I would like to meet with you for 15 minutes to introduce myself."

Do you think this sentence will make them feel good?

Next you have to remember the one reason you are making the call. The goal is to land the appointment, so get right to it! This is where you know the objections will come up and you need to be ready to overcome them. In this situation you cannot eliminate the objections, so embrace them and just be prepared to overcome them.

Below I have listed ones you may get if you are making a cold call to land an appointment.

"I would like to drop by your office to introduce myself."

Now wait for the objection to come…

Objection 1… "I'm too busy."

Response: "With your success that doesn't surprise me but I am not asking for your business today, just an opportunity to meet you."

Objection 2… "I'm already working with someone."

Response: "I appreciate that and I am not asking for your business today, just an opportunity to meet you."

Objection 3… "Please just drop your cards in the mail."

Response: "I would be happy to do that before I leave the office today, but I would still like to meet you face to face, just for 15 minutes."

Objection 4… "Just tell me over the phone."

Response: "I really want to meet with you face to face and shake your hand."

Objection 5… "I'm not interested."

Response: "Meet with me and I'll be brief and not waste your time."

Notice all of my responses are short and to the point. You are not trying to sell, your goal is to get an appointment. It is very rare you will hear more than three objections. Usually you will hear only one or two.

Most people are good people and if you make them feel good at the beginning of the call, be prepared to overcome their objections, be persistent and don't give up. You will have a higher appointment setting ratio.

If you give up after the first "No" cold calling will be challenging for you. This is a sales call and they don't know you. Be prepared to overcome the objections. They will be the same objections that will come up multiple times. It is unlikely you will get a "one off" objection.

Be prepared emotionally for the "No," because it will come. To get to the "Yes" you have to get through the "No." The more calls that turn you down, the more appointments you will set. Knowing and embracing this fact will enable you to get excited for the "No" statement. Once you find out your call ratio, this is when the fun begins! It will now become a game, a race to get to the "Yes."

Can you see how making this a game can actually be fun? You are in sales, aren't you? If you are, you are competitive and turning it into a game will allow you the opportunity to win!

Now when they say, "Yes," be prepared to set the appointment. You want to have two times to suggest.

Tina Mitchell

"Does Monday at 10 a.m. or Wednesday at 1 p.m. work better for you?"

Make it easy for them to respond, and keep your close in mind. Start with a comment that will make them feel good, be ready to overcome the objections, and keep the close in mind. You will have a higher ratio of appointment setting. This is how you "one-time" cold calling!

I will talk more on what to do at the appointment during my *Get Connected* core practice.

Watch for Mistakes

Take control of your mistakes or the mistakes you make will take your business down.

There are a lot of "one-timing" opportunities if you watch for mistakes. When a mistake happens, typically you can implement something into your business model to ensure that mistake does not happen again.

Also, look around the office and monitor others and the mistakes they are making. You will notice they are not "one-off" but instead everyone is making the same mistakes over and over again. When you realize this you will come to the same conclusion that I did. This is a crazy way to run a business so why not change it?

Change how you look at mistakes. View them as a positive because you have the opportunity to find a solution to fix them. Only when you do nothing are they a negative.

Are you constantly putting out fires in your business? Why not eliminate them all together?

Continue to do things the same way and get the same results. If you want different results, you have to make changes.

WATCH for mistakes, LEARN from them and ACT on them.

Another tip: Once you have figured the mistakes out and you feel you have come up with a solution, if it is not working and the mistake continues, you have to try doing something different. You may see the mistake happening less but until it's not happening at all, there is always room for adjusting the solution until you nail it.

If it's not working, don't continue to do it the same way, but find a better way to get the results you want.

Here is a personal example in my mortgage business I can share. There have been statistics that have shown 30% of mortgages do not close on time or fall apart all together because of financing. Why is this? Because the mortgage industry makes the same mistakes over and over again.

One of these areas is communication with the buyers on what to do and what not to do. Why do buyers do this? Because of the lack of communication. I came up with my "8 Tips to a Successful Closing" after monitoring what mistakes buyers were making. This was the first step, to observe.

Next I had to act. I decided to schedule what I call my "Under Contract" meeting. In this meeting I would spend about 30 minutes to go over my 8 tips, one by one and detailing out each one of them. I was confident this would fix the issue. It did make it better, but buyers were still doing what I was coaching them not to do.

I could have blamed it on my client, after all, I was doing my job and I told them what to do and not do. Not only did I tell them but I spend an extra 30 minutes out of my day to review in detail, but I didn't say this. I was not satisfied with my results. I thought there had to be a better way. I had to go back to the drawing board and figure a better way to communicate my 8 tips.

I came to an aha moment. We all know that people will only hear 10-20% of what you say. So now what? Well I came up with a brilliant solution. Don't tell them, just email it to them. So this is what I did.

I still had my "Under Contract" meeting but my 8 tips conversation went from 30 minutes down to 1 minute. I now say, "I am going to email you the most important email you are going to receive during the entire closing process. It is my 8 tips to a success closing. If you follow these tips everything will run efficiently and on time, but if you miss just one of them, your mortgage may not close on time risking your earnest money and worst yet your financing may fall apart all together. It is the most important email you will receive during the entire closing process. All I need from you, is to read my email very carefully and come back to me with any questions. This is a team effort and with your help we will have a successful closing and I will get you into your dream home."

Do you think they will read this email? Do you think they will read with a sense of urgency and detail? Do you think they will now understand 100% of my 8 tips instead of only 10-20% of them? This is how you one-time your mistakes. You have to step back and look again at your solution if you are not getting the results you want.

Make small changes in your business and experience huge results! Remember Thomas Edison and the light bulb? Ten thousand attempts before he got it right.

If you are thinking of purchasing a home, currently under contract, a mortgage professional, or if you're a real estate professional, reach out to me and I will share my 8 Tips to a Successful Closing with you. If you are a real estate professional, you will also want to request a copy of my 8 Tips to a Successful Closing for Realtors.

Ask Questions and Adjust Your Presentation or Client Consultations

Take control of your presentation or your client will take control of the meeting.

Asking questions during your client presentation is a powerful way to "one-time" your business. If one client has a question, it's most likely that question will come up again from a different client. Adjust your presentation to answer that question so it doesn't have to be asked again. This is how you master your presentation and "one-time" it!

If a question comes up, write it down and during your "on-time," "one-time" it! Remember don't interrupt your normal business hours to try to come up with a solution, but instead address it and come up with a solution during your scheduled "on-time."

There are 6 components to a successful presentation…

1. Overview – Explain to your clients what to expect out of the meeting, from what your content will cover to the anticipated result. If

Tina Mitchell

you don't let them know upfront, they will be wondering during the meeting and less able to focus on what you are covering with them.

2. Client Objective – This allows the client time to let you know what they are trying to accomplish. This will allow you to cater your presentation around their needs. It's important to ask specific questions to find out your client's objective. If you don't, the meeting can easily get side tracked and you will no longer be in control of the meeting. There are two reasons it's important for you to control the meeting. You are limited on time and the meeting flow is important.

3. Presentation Content – This is where you go over everything in detail that you said you would cover in step one. This is your presentation content. You will want to strategically schedule break times during your presentation to resolve any questions on what you have covered so far. The best way to ask this is, "From what we have covered so far, do you have any questions?" Silence is good here. Break.... No response is good. The words "so far" are key because you are in the middle of your content and your client will have questions that will be covered later in your presentation. Remember you want to stay on track and in control of the presentation.

If they do have questions, answer them, make note and "one-time" them during your "on-time." Most likely their question is not a "one off" but instead will be ask by multiple clients, if you don't "one-time" it and adjust your presentation to answer this question, it will come up again.

4. Your Unique Proposition – You are not selling your company but instead selling yourself. Everyone has a competitive product, price and process (service). Your client already knows you would not work with a company that did not offer great products. What will sell them on you is your unique proposition. What makes you unique is why they will work with YOU and how you will build a lasting rapport with them.

Stay away from "Product," "Price" and "Process" (service). No three "P's". Sell you and what no one else has. This is your unique proposition.

5. Call To Action – It's important to leave your clients with the next step you need from them. A call to action will ensure your clients are doing what is needed to be successful and that you have a reason to follow up.

You never want to leave a meeting without a call to action. Always have a next step to keep them engaged with you.

Have what I call a "Next Step One Sheet." Your "Next Step One Sheet" will list all the steps you need from your client from A to Z but only give them one call to action at a time. Review them all but keep your client focused on the task at hand.

6. Close – Questions, Find Out What's Important to Them & Ask for Help

Questions

The best way to ask if they have any questions is to prepare a statement similar to this, "From everything that we have covered today, is there anything else you were hoping to get out of our time together that we have not yet discussed?" If they have questions or additional information they were hoping to get out of the meeting, address what they need then write it down. During your "on-time" adjust your presentation to cover this information for your next client. Do not add it if it is a "one off" that most clients would not ask. Most of them will not be a "one off" but instead will be the same questions or needs that multiple clients have, so why not "one-time" them?

This makes sense, doesn't it?

What's important to them?

Ask your client what is important to them. Find out why the product you are offering is important to them.

You want to ask them three times and really drill it down. This is how you go deep and get to the real "why" behind their purchase.

It may sound like this:

"John and Mary, why is home ownership important to you?"

Client Response; "Because we are trying to have a baby and want a home we can call our own."

Your Response: "That is exciting that you are adding to your family. Having your own home vs. renting... What would that mean to you?"

Client Response, "Security."

Your Response, "I agree having security is important. What does security look like for you?"

Client Response, "We want to know that our children will be in a stable neighborhood with a school they know is safe and secure."

Do you see how drilling down what is important to them got to their "why" and how you have now connected on a much deeper level?

Now it's time to ask for their help!

You want to let them know how important introductions to new clients is for your business.

The best way to do this is to give them an example. "John and Mary, just like you... I'm sure you know someone else who can benefit from my expertise."

Also, use an example of someone that may need your service. The best way to do this is give a similar example to them. If they are a renter buying their first home your example may be... "John and Mary, you are currently renters that will soon be reaching your dreams of home ownership, you must (using the word "must" sets the command in their subconscious) have other friends that are renters I can help as well."

Maybe they are buying a vacation home... "John and Mary, now that you are purchasing a vacation home, you must have other friends during this time of their life and they too may be looking for their vacation home."

I always like to use the example of when they purchase a new car. Everyone can relate to this.

"John and Mary, when you purchase a new car and drive it off the lot, because of your new purchase you will see other people on the road driving that same car. Now that you are in need of financing for a new home you will also come across friends, coworkers or family members who are going through the same process as you. When that happens, I

Tina Mitchell

need your help (using the word help is important because it will trigger an emotion in their subconscious and they will want to help you), would you please make an email introduction and include me on the email?"

Let them know exactly how to introduce you so they don't have to think about it. You have spelled it out and they will follow your instructions when the opportunity presents itself.

Use the word "introduction" not "referral." Referral has a sales connotation to it. Introduction is a softer way to ask for their help.

Get a commitment from them upfront and they will feel an obligation to help and will want to do so. The reality is if you don't ask, they may not even think of doing it.

After getting the commitment, give them a day you will follow up if you have not heard from them. On this call you will check in to see if they have ran into anyone that you can help. This may be hard for you to do but remember you are in sales and you have to ask for the business. Also remember their introductions need your service and you are the best person to help them. It's a win-win for both parties.

Involve Your Team

If you have a team, "one-time" your business should be a team effort. I have monthly "one-timing" meetings and the entire team is engaged. Each team member comes prepared with "one-timing" ideas to better their process and/or suggestions for other team members to improve their processes. I track who the "one-timing" idea came from and I will implement or assign it to another team member.

I start each meeting with the previous month's "one-timing" ideas, and we discuss as a team if they worked and if it was the best solution. If not, we go back to the drawing board and keep trying until we get it right. Some "one-timing" ideas are a work in progress and will stay on the list until we nail them.

Always complete the old ideas first before moving to the new ideas.

I had to learn this the hard way and found myself "one-timing" my "one-timing" meeting! I noticed that after our meetings nothing was getting done. When I asked myself why, I realized I was starting with all the new ideas first. This didn't leave any time to discuss the ideas from the previous meeting and there was no accountability to ensure that they were getting resolved. Always start your meeting with the old and complete those before moving on to the new.

During the month the team and I will track… questions, requests, objections and mistakes that came up. We don't discuss them until our monthly "one-timing" meeting because it's important they stay focused on the everyday activities that need to be done to keep the business running. It ensures your team will stay focused. You don't want to interrupt their day to discuss "one-timing" ideas. Just resolve the issue and then during your "one-time" meeting, come up with a solution to "one-time" it so it doesn't happen again.

Can you see how it is necessary to even "one-time" your communication techniques? When and how you communicate to your team is an essential part of the process.

It's important for you to follow this rule too. During normal business hours you too have to stay focused on the everyday activities needed to be done to keep the business running.

See, isn't "one-timing" fun?

Don't you already feel more in control of your business? Can you see how organized your business can be?

As long as you write it down, you can emotionally disconnect from the issue because you know you have a scheduled time that you will "one-time" it. Just make note of the "one-timing" opportunity and get back to business.

Use Technology

Use the tools that technology has created for you. You will experience "one-timing" results with the least amount of effort. The most important tool to have is a Customer Relationship Management system or CRM. This is a database that manages your clients, referral partners and opportunities. A CRM will also manage your system and processes. If you don't have one, I highly recommend that you take time to implement one. It will have the greatest return on investment. If you want to "one-time" your business you can't effectively do it without a CRM.

Remember, watch for questions, requests, objections and mistakes and you, too, will experience the "one-timing" magic.

Tina Mitchell

CHAPTER 11 - IDEAS TO ONE-TIME YOUR BUSINESS

Commit to Time Blocking

Take control of your time or your time will control your business and your life.

Create your time-blocker and stick to it. Here are a few critical things you must have on your time-blocker if you are in sales.

- **Get Started.** Get motivated, review and prioritize list of tasks you will do.
- **Return calls and emails.** 2 to 3 blocks a day - Make sure you always have blocked to return calls and emails at the beginning of your day and at the end of your day. You can have blocked times during the day, too.
- **Generate new business.** Power Hour - Power Hour is for phone calls. Do things differently than your competitors and pick up the phone. This is a must if you want to build lasting partnerships. I will talk in more detail about this when I cover my *Get Connected* professional core practice.
- **Meet with potential new clients.** Client consultations.
- **Meet with new or existing referral partners.** Meetups or meet & greets.
- **Touch Points** Writing thank you cards and social medial posts. When using social media it's important to comment on your target partner lists or client posts not just post your own thoughts.

- **Work on your business.** The daily activities you must do to keep your business running. Go to your list reviewed during your "get started" for the day

- **Close your day.** Set up tasks to be completed tomorrow.

Time management is really self management. Hold yourself accountable, stick to your schedule and follow through.

You will notice there is no "working" "on your business" as this is reserved for your once a month "on-time." I believe education and research should be reserved for your "on-time." Remember you can do extra "on-time" during your "off-time" (personal time). Time-blocking is critically important in any industry. If you have a team, they must also be time blocked.

You have to schedule time with yourself and keep these appointments. They are the most important ones to your business. If you are in sales, anytime you have the urge to cancel time you have for yourself "working on your business" or "working in your business," ask yourself if you had an appointment scheduled with another client would you cancel this appointment for another client's need? The answer should be no. So, why would you do this during the time you have scheduled with yourself? This time is more important as it is not about one client but is about your future business. You have to value this time more than any other time. Keep your commitments to yourself as you do with your clients.

What if you need to make sales calls to generate new business? (Power Hour) If during this blocked time you always are interrupted with other clients that may request your service now, when do you ever generate new business? Your clients will respect the time limitation you give them and if they do not, they are a "one-off" client and you need

Tina Mitchell

to let them go. They are not the clients you want to build your business around.

If you do not block your day in any of these categories, you are telling yourself they are not a priority and are not important to your business. Ask yourself is generating new business important? Of course the answer is, "yes." Run an efficient day and your business will produce the results you want. Let your business run you and remain on the hamster wheel, in the rat race and consistently putting out fires. Can you see how important time blocking really is to your business?

Check Lists: Everything we do has a list or steps. Why not create check lists to keep you and your team on task?

There is no such thing as multitasking. Or, if there is, it's the ability to be working on one project, stopping in the middle to move to another project, then moving back to the original project, and picking up effortlessly where you left off, not missing a beat. This would be multitasking. You can't work on two things at one time unless it's talking and walking; this would be an exception to the rule. Or is it? Even walking and talking at the same time is difficult or at least talking and driving is. We have all seen those studies.

I don't believe that you should work on one task, stop in the middle and go back to the other task. I just want to provide my description of multitasking but don't believe in doing it.

Studies have shown that when trying to multitask you lose 28 percent of the average work day. What would your business look like if you were 28 percent more productive during your day? I came up with the saying "one-tasking." This is what I do and train my team to do as well. Work on one task at a time, finish it and then move onto the next task.

The other important part of managing your tasks is to work on the most difficult task first. When pushing them aside, you will continue to do so and they will not get done in a timely manner. Not only this, but the emotional stress that is added to your day knowing these tasks need to be done but they have not, will also affect your productivity.

Email Templates: It's easy to start creating email templates. Anytime you write an email, ask yourself if you would ever need this email again. In most situations the answer will be yes. Instead of deleting the email, you should save it as a template to use for the next time. Why continue to recreate the same emails over and over again?

Email Tips

Take control of your email or your email will control your day.

Tip 1: Group emails - Most email services will allow you to group. This puts all communication into one email grouped based on the subject line. If you don't do this your email will be disorganized and can't be manage effectively. Just ask yourself how many emails go back and forth in one conversation and how efficient it would be if they were grouped into one? Have you ever caught yourself responding to an email only to realize you responded to an old part of the conversation as the conversation moved forward before you saw it? This is because you are not grouping your emails.

Tip 2: Mass emails - Send mass emails at the end of your business day. If you don't, you will get responses throughout the day and this will interrupt your blocked time for other tasks. In the morning you can respond to all of them during your morning blocked time to do so.

Tina Mitchell

Tip 3: Don't scan emails - Only look at emails during your blocked time. If you scan them, you will want to respond and will interrupt what you are currently working on and this is not an efficient way to manage your email or your day.

Tip 4: Shut off email alerts - I know this may seem hard but I promise it is worth it and will change your business. Stay focused on the task at hand.

Tip 5: Last name in subject line - Put your clients last name in the subject line. This will enable you to manage your emails and to group at a glance based on last name.

Tip 6: Subject line consistency - Keep all standard email template subject lines consistent based on topic. As with Tip 5, this will help you group and manage your emails with the highest efficiency.

Tip 7: Stop the email confusion madness - If you are noticing an email conversation going back and fourth because of communication confusion, pick up the phone and discuss voice to voice to get clarification.

Tip 8: Scan & delete spam first - During your scheduled email time when you open your email, first scan through them looking for (spam) emails. Delete them and mark as spam as not to receive them again.

Tip 9: Create folders - Folders are for emails you have already addressed but want to keep for future use. The key is to keep your in-box clean. Make sure you fully complete what is needed so you do not forget about something. Once completed, always move the email into the appropriate folder for future use if you think you may need it again.

All email services have a search function that allow you to quickly search for any email in any folder you may be looking for.

Tip 10: Marketing folder - One of your folders should be for marketing ideas. Don't read or do anything with these emails, just move to your folder. These should only be read during your "on-time." Some will be great ideas you will implement, but others will not and you will delete. Regardless, reading these emails will take valuable time that will prevent you from staying focused on what you are currently working on. Your email time-blocked time will quickly turn into idea time and this is only reserved for your "on-time!"

Tip 11: Cc yourself on sent emails - If you are having a conversation with someone and it has not been resolved, cc yourself on your reply. This works perfectly when you are grouping your emails as mentioned in Tip 1.

Tip 12: Sort emails with oldest first - You naturally want to see the most recent emails but when you do this, you keep putting off the emails that need your attention. Sort based on the oldest first so you can train yourself not to keep pushing them off. You have to address them, so why not get to it. The idea that a client expects to have an immediate response is not true. If they do, maybe you need different clients.

Tip 13: Set up email rules - This will enable you to set up in advance what you would like particular email notifications to do.

Tip 14: Set up followup.com - This service allows you to set up email reminders based on whether your recipients are responding to your email as requested. The name of the game is to keep your inbox clear!

There will be "one-off" times when something urgent is happening and you need to monitor your email, however be careful to ensure it is really urgent. Once you "one-time" your business, you will have very few urgencies that will arise.

Email is a great tool but if not managed effectively, it can be devastating to your business efficiency.

Voice Mail:

The first step is to change your voicemail daily. It's nice for a client to hear a new message every day. Once you create a habit to change your voicemail once a day, go to the next level and mention on your voicemail specific times you will be returning calls during your time-blocked time to do so.

You can also have fun with your voice mail. Maybe a market update. Is it a sunny day? Make mention of that. Is your favorite sports team playing? Mention that! Is it a holiday? Say happy holiday!

Online Calendar:

An online calendar can make it easier for your clients to schedule a meeting with you. This will prevent the back and forth emails to coordinate schedules.

A great service I use for my online calendar is Setster, but there are many on the market from which to choose.

You can also put the link to your on-line calendar in your email signature. Wouldn't it be a nice surprise to see you have a new appointment without having to request it?

I have referral partners that when meeting with clients they take them right to my calendar and have them schedule a time to meet with me. An online calendar is a great way to "one-time" your appointment setting.

Web Conferencing:

This makes it convenient to jump online with your client to view your computer screen as you go through your presentation. You also can be on video for more of a face to face effect. People are busy and commute times can make in-person visits difficult. Think about how you may be able to use web meetings with your clients. Eliminate the location challenge. You can now work with anyone who is located anywhere.

GoToMeeting or Join.me are both great to use for client web meetings.

On-line Forms:

There are times when you need information from your clients to prepare for a presentation or meeting.

What questions do you need to know to prepare for the meeting?

A great product I use for my online forms is FormSite. Google forms is another great product.

Task Manager

How are you going to manage all of your new great "one-timing" ideas? A task manager can manage all the ideas and tasks in your business. It will manage the projects you are working on. It is also great to keep your team on task and accountable for the tasks that are needed to be completed. A great resource to look into is Asana.

Tina Mitchell

Scripts:

To have a script is not to sound "scripted," but instead to be prepared upfront on how you would like to deliver a message to your client to ensure they understand what you need from them to guarantee a successful outcome.

Have you ever had a conversation with a client and then realized the words didn't come out right? You are having the same conversations over and over again. Why not be prepared and provide a powerful message?

This is the power of scripts!

Blog:

When one client asks a question, this is usually a great topic to write a blog on. Most likely other potential clients could benefit from reading this blog post. Your blog becomes your own personal library that clients can read and stay connected with you.

Video:

There is no better way to deliver a message than with a video. It can be a simple video taken from your desk or a more advanced one in a Green Screen studio. This is the best way to connect on more of a personal level with your clients and referral partners, outside of face to face. BombBomb is a great resource to create videos right from your phone.

I committed to using videos after attending a workshop where the presenter made a profound comment. I was sitting with hundreds of other business professionals and you know when a speaker says something and it is as if he or she is looking right at you as if you were the only one in the entire room?

Well, this is how I felt, as if a spotlight was shining on me, and not in a good way. This obviously was not the case, but it sure felt like it. He said, "Have you ever seen yourself on video and saw all your flaws, thinking you look terrible on video?" He went on to say, "Get over it, this is what you look like when you are face to face with your clients." This was the moment; I got over it, and committed to using video.

If you see me on video you will notice when I talk my mouth goes crooked and the more excited and passionate I get when communicating my message it gets even more crooked. Well, this is how it looks when I'm face to face as well. It is my uniqueness and I have decided to embrace it, instead of seeing it as a flaw. What about those wrinkles? Well we have them when we are face to face too, don't we? (I stated "we" not to leave myself out, because I have them too.) Embrace your imperfections and get comfortable on video!

Note Taking

When you attend workshops, go to seminars or meetings, how do you take notes? If you handwrite them using a notepad, you then also have to transfer your notes somewhere. If you don't, when going back to review later, you may have lost them or you will have to sift through your notes to find the ones you are looking for. Why not "one-time" your note taking and use your iPad. There are a lot of note applications available to keep your note taking organized. Evernote is a great resource and it is free.

You can even do voice recording with your devices. Remember when I shared about my little black book? The book where I wrote all my thoughts down. Remember how I shared how I had to pull over on the side of the road as not to forget my words? Well I have even "one-timed" how I take down my thoughts. I now use a voice recording application to take all my thoughts down. No more pulling over on the side of the freeway. Thank goodness!

"One-timing" Benefits for Your Business

Build a business model that is efficient, consistent and replicable.

- ▸ Efficiency will produce a business model that maximizes your efforts in the least amount of time.

- ▸ Consistency assures that your business model provides the results you want.

- ▸ Replicable assures that your business model is sustainable and can be duplicated effortlessly.

Even as a waitress I quickly learned how to run an efficient shift. Did you know that if you tip sugar upside down and roll the packets of sugar back and forth on the palm of your hand it will even the sugar and make room for twice as many packets in the sugar holder? This was helpful when working double shifts as I didn't have to fill the holders twice.

I was always working "both ways." This is what I called it when I trained other servers. Why would you ever walk your station without picking up empty plates on your way back to the kitchen? I never went empty handed going to or from my station.

See, you can even "one-time" your business in the restaurant industry. It works in any industry.

It's in the small changes in your business where you will experience huge results!

If you're not "one-timing your business," you're doing the same tasks multiple times and duplicating your efforts.

Remember the two books that were the inspiration behind my "one-time your business" philosophy? <u>Who Moved My Cheese</u> by Spencer Johnson and <u>The Compound Effect</u> by Darren Hardy. Both of these books have the same message but explained in a different way. The importance of change! "One-time your business" is about change, too, and shared in my own unique way.

Be progressive not regressive. Be willing to make change. Don't just say, "It's working the way it is." Instead ask yourself, "What can I do to make it better?"

What would our world look like if no one was willing to look at things differently and make change? Could you imagine life without planes, cars, cells phones and computers? Maybe it wouldn't be so bad because we would not know what we were missing, but I'm glad these people looked at the opportunity to change the world.

Look at change as an opportunity, not an obligation. Change your mindset. To "one-time your business" is a mindset to make change.

Run your business. Don't let your business run you!

Tina Mitchell

CHAPTER 12 - Embrace Your Strengths

"Embrace your strengths and live a successful personal and professional life."

- Tina Mitchell

To be the best "you" in your professional life, you must define your strengths and put all your focus on them.

Your weaknesses are things you will need to hire out.

We all know that you need a "To Do List" but I feel it is just as important, that you have a "Not to Do List." On this list are the things you are not good at or just don't want to do.

If you look at the most successful people, they focus on their strengths. Not only will you be more successful, but you will enjoy what you do.

Just as one of my personal core practices is *Learn To Fail* (realizing that life is balanced), there is no difference here.

We have to admit that we are balanced too. We have strengths and weaknesses. Learn what your strengths are, as this is the key to enjoying your professional and personal life. You can't enjoy what you do when you are doing everything, because you are not good at everything.

Focus on finding your own strengths. Think about what comes naturally to you and is easy for you to do. Don't choose attributes that you admire in others. This can take you down the wrong path of following your weaknesses, not your strengths.

I have listed below some questions to help you determine your strengths and weaknesses.

Strengths

What are your real talents?

What do you enjoy doing?

What could you do and not get paid?

What can you do for hours and it doesn't seem like work?

What are things that people come to you and ask for your help?

What do you offer to help others with?

What do you want to learn more about?

What things come easy to you?

Weaknesses

What do you procrastinate doing?

What gives you stress thinking about having to do it?

What tasks make you anxious?

What do you lose sleep over?

What things fall through the cracks?

Where are mistakes made on a regular basis?

What do you avoid doing?

What things are hard for you to focus on?

Don't get confused with lack of confidence. Remember you have to be willing to fail to reach your true potential. You have to be willing to take risks and get out of your comfort zone to grow. Lack of confidence and being stressed about a task are completely different.

Tina Mitchell

If I didn't step out of my comfort zone, you would not be reading my book right now. When my friends (some who have shared their thoughts at the end of my book) encouraged me to write a book and tell my story, my first thought was, "no way." I thought, "I'm not a writer and I could never do this." I then thought deeper and heard my friends' voices in my head saying, "Do it!"

Since I embrace my strengths and hire out my weaknesses, I hired my editor, Jen, thinking I would just record my voice telling her my story and she could put my words into writing. After my first interview with Jen that weekend, I sat down at my computer and started typing. I didn't get up from my chair except for a couple of small breaks. I worked from morning to late in the evening. I guess since it was actually until 2 or 3 a.m., I would have to say I worked from morning to morning. I then took a short nap and went back at it.

I repeated this process for many weekends to follow. I couldn't step away and stop writing. I don't know how many times I read my book from cover to cover to add more, change words and to really embrace the experience. I wanted to express my words in type the best way I could.

After all was said and done, my book is 97% word for word mine. I am so proud of myself as I would have never thought I could do this. My editor started to make changes but I asked her to go back to my words because I wanted you, my reader, to read my words. The best thing about this process for me was I really enjoyed writing and telling my story. If I had not followed my internal navigation that was telling me to write, I would have miss out on this experience and today you would be reading someone else's words and not my words. I may have not written as a professional writer, but they are my words and I am proud of them.

You don't want to miss an opportunity to embrace your strengths when it may feel as if it is a weakness. As I have stated earlier, listen to what your body is telling you, it will not steer you wrong.

When you do determine a weakness, why spin your wheels trying to be good at everything when the reality is you cannot? You have to be willing to hire out – the old saying, "spend money to make money" – is part of this. Determine the cost to hire a team to do what you don't want to do or what you are not good at.

How much more income could you earn if you only focused on what you are good at? What would your life look like if you didn't have to do things you did not want to do?

It doesn't have to be a long process to figure out what your strengths are. It's actually very simple. All you have to do is make note of things that you don't enjoy doing. If you track this in your current professional environment you can have it nailed in 30 days by just monitoring and making note of them. Just as in your personal passions, your body is like a navigation system and will guide you through your professional strengths and weaknesses. You need to listen to what your body is telling you. You will find that even some of the simplest tasks you will not want to do.

Remember my strawberry picking story...

I shared with you that I reached my dream and was the #1 berry picker and named Strawberry Picking Season Champion! What I didn't tell you is how I did it. I embraced my strengths!

After a couple days of picking I realized, that sheer will and desire was not going to help me reach my goal. My tiny legs were no match against the other older workers I was competing against. If I was going to reach my dream, I had to think differently, strategize, and play it smart.

I approached another boy on the field, one who could run fast, and offered to share my earnings. I was paid $1.20 a flat and I offered to pay him 40 cents of that. His job was to be my runner. He would gather the empty flats for me. As I filled the flats with berries he would run them down the aisle to be counted, allowing me more time to pick. He had the easiest job because he didn't even have to pick the strawberries. While I did all of the hard work, he could rest.

This was my idea because I didn't want to pay more than 40 cents a flat, he didn't want to work hard and I knew I could pick the berries faster, so it was a great deal for both of us. Since I was super-fast at collecting berries, but not strong enough to carry the heavy flats filled with the berries, I knew I had to make that task of picking my focus. It was my first season berry picking, but I had a dream and I knew it could happen if I worked hard and smart. The only problem was the next day that boy did not show up on the bus. I had to find another one to take his place. I can't count how many boys I had to go though. After a day, most never wanted to come back. Why would they? It was summer and they had better things to do with their time.

Day after day I repeated this process until one day I reached the end of the season and it was time for the official counts to be tallied. I had earned a lot of money that summer (even with sharing my proceeds), but I anxiously waited for my dream to become a reality. Like the sweetness of the berries, I could already taste it and it happened! I embraced my strength, hired out my weakness and took the prize.

Even though I was small, young and not strong, I won because I was smart, strategized and worked hard.

Embrace your strengths and hire out your weaknesses.

I never understood why some parents focus on their children's F's instead of focusing on their A's.

My mom taught my sister and me to love learning. However when I struggled with a subject, emphasis was not placed on that subject. Instead I was encouraged in the activities and talents where I could excel. It taught my sister and me to move towards our strengths and use them to overcome areas of weakness.

What is an easy task that you just keep pushing off?

This doesn't necessarily mean you're not good at this task, but it's just something you don't want to do. It's okay. You just need to hire someone to do it for you, to be successful and have a life worth living.

Think for a moment how devastating pushing these tasks aside would be to your business. Easy or not, they have to be done and done in a prompt manner.

Now, think if you hired someone to do these for you, what would your business look like? More important, what would your life look like?

I was recently at a business growth retreat with some of my Realtor partners. The facilitator went around the room and asked each of us to share. I had shared how I hired out my weaknesses. I went on to explain how I disliked all the processes. My Realtor friends were shocked to hear this. They said, "But you are a process guru?" I replied,

Tina Mitchell

"This could not be further from the truth. My strength is building the system and I hire out the task of working the processes. I design, observe and improve the processes and then delegate working the tasks of the process." If the processes were left to me, my business would surely fail! This is the benefit of embracing your strengths. To those on the outside, even your weaknesses will shine as your strengths. Can you see how powerful it is to embrace your strengths?

When I was the lounge manager at the Holiday Inn, I was a one-woman-show. Once I built up my clientele it was too much for me to cover on my own. The natural solution was to hire a server to run the floor, but I knew this was not maximizing my strengths. I wouldn't enjoy just standing behind the bar making cocktails and my clients would not have liked this either. I had built the relationships with my clients and I needed to do what I did best - mingle and interact with them. So my solution was to hire a runner, someone who would run the food out to the tables and run the empty plates back to the kitchen. I never left the lounge but instead worked the room. I shared my tips, but it was worth it as I was strategic with the tasks I delegated.

With my Mortgage software, I definitely don't want to sell software, so I had to hire a sales team to do it for me. This allows me to continue working at a high level in my mortgage practice as well as run my software company.

In my mortgage business, I am the face of my business and the conversations with my clients and referral partners. The back end of the business that I don't enjoy doing is handled by my team. I always say, "my team is the drive behind the effort." I am "the rainmaker" and decision maker. This is my asset to the team and my strengths lie here.

I GET the business and my team DRIVES the business.

I have clients and referral partners ask me all the time "how do you do it all?" my answer "I don't!" It looks as if I do because I am accessible and available. This is because all the behind the scenes is covered by my team. I love what I do because I do what I love!

Do you really have time to do everything? You may say, "I can do it better than anyone else." The reality is that there are only so many hours in the day. If you try doing it all yourself your business will suffer. You will not have enough hours in the day and things will fall through the cracks, you will burn yourself out, or your personal and family life will suffer. All three of these are at risk of happening and how stressful would that be for your business and your life?

Do you say, "I would do this task for free" or "they could not pay me enough to do this task." How damaging could it be to your business if you don't hire out the tasks you don't want to do?

Does this make sense to you? Can you see the benefit of hiring a team?

Are you in sales like me? If you are, you need time to connect. This is my third professional core practice and I will talk in more detail about this later. You need to make time to connect.

Allow for failure as life is balanced and so are people. Ask yourself this question, "If you did everything, would you do it **all** perfectly?"

As long as you have an accountability system in place, this allows you to step in and train around any issues that may come up.

When you build a team, you need to follow 3 principles.

Tina Mitchell

Team, Accountability and Recognition. These are my Core Leadership Practices. I do not discuss these in detail in my book but here is a simple way to describe them…

Team: build an environment where everyone is a part of the team and feel as though they are a strong contributor to the team's success… because they are.

Accountability: You must have an accountability system in place. As the leader you need to know everything that is happening in the business. You need to know when it's necessary for you to step in.

Recognition: This goes hand in hand with accountability. You can't recognize a team member if you don't have an accountability system in place. Recognition is important to allow your team members to thrive and be excited about being a part of the team's success. I don't believe in mixing job positions. Every team member has very specific and individual roles. The roles do not cross over with other team member's roles.

How can you have accountability when the team roles overlap? How can anyone be recognized if their roles are not clearly defined and defined on an individual basis?

Yes, I do believe that you have to cross train, but the individual day to day tasks and activities need to be clearly defined and understood by each team member. This includes you as the leader. The worst thing you can do as the leader is get into what I call your team's "lane." You need to stay in your own "lane" and out of theirs, unless it is really necessary to step in and fix an issue or coach them on mastering their craft.

Think about how this applies to driving. If the other drivers do not stay in their own lane, deadly disasters would result. This can happen in business if everyone doesn't remain in their own lane.

It is also important that you allow them to take ownership of their position. Encourage and allow them to make suggestions to improve their roles. They are working the position and will have valuable input on how to improve it. They will feel more attached to the outcome when they have a part in the decision of how their position is run.

Remember life is balanced and your team will fail (as you do). They will only be successful if you allow them the opportunity to fail. If you were doing their job and yours too, would you fail? Of course you would! Allow them to fail, too. Set up the roles, monitor, adjust and train when needed.

In every operation you have the "business" and the "process." The business brings in the money and the process ensures the money continues to come in.

In every operation you have a "leader" and a "team."

The leader works the business and the team works the process.

If my production drops, it drops for two reasons; I'm not doing my job "working the business" or I'm getting tangled up in the team's job of "working the process." There can be many reasons this is happening, but only one solution, **fix it**.

As the leader, stay focused on "working the business."

Every business will also have a "system." As the leader you set up the system, and then get to "business."

Of course there are times you have to step in to fix or adjust the "system" or "process" but once you do this, get back to business!

How to Hire…

Don't hire for personal reasons, hire for practical reasons. Don't hire someone like you; hire someone that can excel at what you can't.

There are great resources to determine your potential hire's strengths. You know yourself but you can't tell what your potential hires are good at without testing them.

- ▸ Myers Briggs
- ▸ Clifton StrengthsFinder
- ▸ Wiley DiSC Assessment
- ▸ AVA Activity Vector Analysis

Use one of these resources to assist you before hiring.

Different job duties require a particular personality traits. Learn if your potential hire has the traits needed to be successful in that position.

Make your hire, the right hire, the first time around. This will save you a lot of stress and grief in your business.

Working interviews are also an essential part of the hiring process.

Caller or Dialer Position

Provide a script in the interview and have the candidate call. There is no warning or preparation for this test.

Watch their body language after you give them the instructions. One of two things will happen. They will slouch down as if they are going to fall underneath the desk, or they will perk up and sit up tall, ready for the challenge. It will be obvious if this is a strength or weakness for them and if they are right for the position.

Does the position need presentation skills?

This test cannot be spontaneous because you need to give them time to prepare. Give them a topic with no other instructions and let them take it from there. This will require them to get creative. They will have to do all the research on the topic, decide if they want visuals and decide how they want to structure the presentation.

Do they ask questions during their presentation or not? Do they make charts or provide statistics? Watch the way they present without instruction from you, let them figure it out and see their creativity.

Does the position require networking?

Bring them to a networking event with you and observe how they interact. One of two things will most likely happen in this test. The candidate will stay close to you and have minimal conversations or they will venture out on their own and mingle. It will be obvious if they have the strengths needed to help you grow your business.

Are math skills needed?

This is a simple one. Give them a math quiz.

Will they be doing a lot of communication on your behalf?

Give them a grammar quiz, and/or a writing prompt, so you can see their writing abilities.

What software do they have to be familiar with?

If Excel, have them build an Excel worksheet.

If PowerPoint, have them create a presentation.

In my mortgage business, a working interview is fun because I can utilize a case study. I can easily see if they have the skills needed to assist in structuring a loan. I give them a case study during the working interview and watch the outcome. Case studies are great for a lot of businesses.

You get the point.

Working interviews can save you from making the wrong hire.

The wrong hire will cost you time, money and energy. Make the hire the right one the first time!

The hiring process should take time. Do not rush the process, but instead take time to find the right person for the position you are hiring for.

It's rare that people can improve upon their weaknesses. If they do, you still haven't solved the problem, they most likely will not be happy in their position as it is not their strength and they will fail or quit. This can be a hiring nightmare and unfair to your candidate. Do you really want to do this to them? Hire smart!

Why spend energy trying to improve what you're not good at? Instead, do what comes easy. You will be amazed how much you can get done, what you can accomplish and how much you will love what you do.

Are you wasting your time trying to improve your weaknesses while losing valuable time getting better at your strengths?

To reach your true potential it's critical to focus on your strengths. This doesn't mean you should stay in your comfort zone. As I mentioned earlier, you have to be willing to fail in order to grow; however, you want to fail in the directions of your strengths, not fail trying to improve your weaknesses.

Most people who are intent to improve themselves focus on getting better at what they are not good at. At best, you may become adequate. This is backwards. Improve on what you know you are good at! Be intentional and not just to be good, but to be the best! This is possible if you focus on your strengths.

Don't try being someone you are not, but instead embrace the person you are! Success will be yours!

Pay attention to the opportunities and the problems.

The opportunities are moving toward your strengths.

The problems are moving toward your weaknesses, and it's time to hire out.

Now that you have found the right person for the job and have hired them, you must be ready for them. Have your system, processes, and plan in place.

Tina Mitchell

In absence of a system, your team will make up their own. Do you want control of your business or do you want to leave the control to your team?

In absence of a process, your team will not follow one. Do you want your team to wing it?

In absence of a plan, your team will flounder. Do you want your team productive or destructive?

You are the leader and you need to lead with your system, your process, and your plan.

If you are not in a position to hire, try teaming up with someone, hire a virtual assistant or get help through Elance. Another option is finding an intern.

Partnering with someone can be great, but it can also fail very easily. It's hard to have two leaders. I could not do this, but I have witnessed successful partnerships. I have also witnessed many more fail, so be careful. To have a successful partnership you must plan upfront every detail of every role. Who will be doing what? Who is responsible for what results? What results are expected? Who makes decisions for what part of the business? If these are not clearly defined upfront, the partnership will fail.

Remember my earlier advice, you and your team must remain in your own lane? Well it's no different with a partnership. You most both stay in your own lane for the partnership to survive. A partnership should mean both of you are experts in your own right. If not, it's not worth partnering. You must partner with someone that excels in your weaknesses and you in theirs.

A virtual assistant or (VA) is very inexpensive. There are companies that act as the recruiter for you. They already have a group of VAs that you can select from. They have gone through the DISC profile that I talked about when hiring a team member. VAs have all levels of experience in many different job functions.

What would your business look like if you just hired one for 20 hours a week? You can find companies with rates as low as $10 an hour which costs $200 a week. There are other companies with rates much higher so shop around. My OutDesk is a great company to look into especially if you are a real estate professional, as they specialize in them.

How could your business change with this minimal fee? VAs have a wide range of abilities; from cold calls to generate opportunities, to researching things you just don't have time to do or reporting that you hate to do, to paperwork and so much more. Some VAs are from other countries and are eager to please and and are happy to have the opportunity and have the job. The accountability is managed through the company contracting them. To retain employment, they need to excel in their positions or the company will replace them for you!

Elance is another resource. Elance is a vendor management system (VMS) for contractors and third-party services. You can post jobs, search for freelance professionals, and solicit proposals. Once a contractor is selected, communications and files are exchanged through the Elance system. Payment can either be an hourly rate or paid per project through Elance's system. Just as with a VA, there are all levels of experience in many different job functions.

You may also find that hiring an intern is a good fit for your business. In some cases you will pay your intern, and in others, you will not. If you do not, be sure you consult with legal counsel to ensure you are within your state law.

It's not about being the best at everything, but instead being smart enough to admit what you are not good at. Don't let your ego stand in your way of success and allowing you to enjoy your professional and personal life.

Be great at a few things. Don't try to master all things.

Are you in the right profession? Is your career allowing you to work within your strengths? How do you know this?

This too is easy. Just track and monitor as above. The difficulty will be if you realize you are in the wrong profession.

What then?

You have to MAKE A CHANGE.

Life is too short.

Embrace what you are good at and love what you do.

Do you live to work or do you work to live?

It's a risk to start over but if you make the leap, take the risk and follow through, allowing yourself to fail (because you will), in the long term, you will be successful if you're passionate about what you do.

Pay attention to how you wake up in the morning. This is a good indicator if you are embracing your strengths or trying to correct your weaknesses. Do you feel energized and excited for your day or do you keep hitting the snooze button and just want to go back to sleep?

Do what you want to do, love to do, and are good at doing. Hire out the rest!

We are often told to focus on improving our weaknesses. I suggest you focus on mastering your strengths!

CHAPTER 13 - GET CONNECTED

"Connect with people on a deeper level and they will want to support your business and your life."

- Tina Mitchell

Being an entrepreneur can be an exciting venture, but it can be a lonely and unsuccessful one if you don't connect with others.

Get to know other people instead of trying to get them to know you. This is how you get past the surface connection and build lasting connections.

Time is limited; choose wisely how you spend it and who you spend it with!

To build and maintain relationships you must truly connect with people. The key to a successful business is based on the connections you make over time. The best relationships don't happen quickly but you have to work on them, foster them and take care of them.

To build stronger relationships; listen more so you can find out what's important to them. Ask for feedback, so you can continue to build on your relationships. Have a routine to follow up and stay connected.

Your professional life is about connecting with others. It is essential to being successful in business. It's not just enough to have a great product, price and service, you also need to connect.

Sell who you are, not what you have, and connect on a deeper level. As I mentioned earlier, lead with your unique proposition and your product, price and processes (service) will be secondary. You never want to lead with the three "P's."

You want to connect on a personal level. Once you can do this, your clients, referral partners and colleagues will want to help you. Building a business or great working environment is the same as building a friendship or relationship. It takes time and it's important to connect on a personal level. Find out what is important to them and they will want to find out what is important to you. They will also want to help you succeed.

It's important in any business to connect. When you are looking for work; who do you need to connect with to get the job you want? When you are in sales; who do you need to connect with to get the business? When you are part of a team; who do you need to connect with to ensure that you have the support you need to be successful in your position?

When I started my mortgage business and knew nothing about a very complex and complicated industry, if I didn't connect, I would have never made it. Why did my colleagues want to help me succeed? Why did the support team want to support me? Why did my referral partners give me a chance? Because I got connected with them and found out what was important to them.

I talked about the 80/20 rule earlier. This principle also applies when getting connected.

80% of your sales come from 20% of your customers. Who are you paying attention too?

Tina Mitchell

Spend 80% of your time connecting with 20% of your clients.

You want to connect with people in your own industry, but most of your time you should be connecting with people that can support what you do.

As a mortgage professional there are a lot of events to connect with other mortgage professionals and as fun as this is, it is not the best use of my time. I have to decide where to focus most of my time. I use the 80/20 rule and 80% of the events I attend are Realtor events and 20% are mortgage events. Why? Because Realtors support my business. Sales workshops are the same in any industry but I attend ones that are for Realtor professionals, not Mortgage professionals. Better yet, I invite my Realtors to attend with me. I will spend the other 20% with Mortgage professionals and interacting in my own industry.

Choose to get connected and build lasting connections.

Build respect and people will value you and want to be a part of what you are doing.

Build trust and people will want to work with you.

Be memorable and people will remember you.

Be your unique self. It's not about being like everyone else but shining as an individual.

I don't believe in adjusting my personality to connect with the people that may be able to support my business. I believe in being who I am and attracting the people I should be connecting with, people who are like me. It takes no effort to be who you are but it takes a lot of energy to try to change who you are to attract others not like you.

There are enough people in the world to find people like you.

It's easy to be the person you are; it's hard to try to be someone you are not.

It feels better to be your honest self rather then trying to be a fake you.

Make a list of people you want to connect with. Find out everything you can about them. What clients they cater to, how they get their business, who they are currently working with, their family, what they enjoy doing and what's important to them. This will help you determine if they may be a good fit for you. Do they align with you and your business? Be strategic when choosing who you want to meet and possibly work with. Preparation upfront will save time and energy.

If they are true partners and the right partners, they will also become your friends. Do you love golf? Why not find business partners that love golf too? Do you want to work with builders? Find the people that also focus on builders? Are you a mother with young children? Why not work with other professional mothers with young children? Do you have a strong faith? Why would you not work with others that share your faith?

Choose your business partners like you choose your friends. Same interests and same values. People like you.

This makes sense doesn't it? It would make working more fun wouldn't it? You would be more successful in business wouldn't you?

Tina Mitchell

My personal core practices are a big part of who I am so I want to work with other professions that are passionate about personal growth as well. They are a perfect fit for me and I am for them. I have built some of my closest friendships with them. Many of them have contributed to my life and I to theirs. Some are mentioned at the end of my book and have shared their thoughts for you to read.

Networking events are an important part of connecting with people. Just as above, attending events helps you meet the people who can support your business. It's a great place to get connected and hear what is interesting to them and their business. For me that means connecting with Realtors at professional networking events.

Time is limited, so choose carefully which networking events you attend. Network with the list you made. If you are attending, connect with the people you want to meet. Be strategic about who you want to talk with. Try to sit next to one or more of those people on your list.

Come prepared to the networking event. How will you be introducing yourself? What is your 10 second commercial? I really believe 30 seconds is too long. 10 seconds is all you need for a power statement of who you are and what you do. Most important is to make sure your commercial is about "you" not your company and explains why you are unique. Be sure to add something to your commercial that is unforgettable so you are memorable.

Three steps to writing your 10 second commercial

1. Who are you?
2. What do you do?
3. What is your hook?

If you have a more detailed conversation you can then share your unique proposition. The "hook" is what will keep your commercial short, sweet and memorable.

Examples...

"Hi, my name is Mary Brown and I help businesses with their promotional products. If you want your clients to remember you, just remember me."

"Hi, my name is Mary Brown and I own a catering business. Little or small, I cater to them all."

"Hi, my name is Mary Brown and I am a financial adviser. A doctor saves lives, I save lifestyles."

My 10 second commercial...

"Hi, my name is Tina Mitchell and I'm a mortgage professional. I finance dreams." This is my "hook" when meeting with clients.

"Hi, my name is Tina Mitchell and I'm a mortgage professional. I help realtors take control of their business so it no longer controls them." This is my "hook" when meeting with Realtors.

Sound familiar?

This is my quote from my first professional core practice, *One-time Your Business*.

This is different from any of my competitors, has nothing to do with my product, price or service and has a hook that is unique to me. Also, it always starts a conversation. They want to know more. A common response is, "How do you help Realtors take control of their business?" Now the fun begins, I can start a conversation, a meaningful conversation and connect with them. While connecting with them I make sure to use this time to really get to know who they are and what is important to them. Do you think when I follow up with a call after the networking event I will get the appointment?

Make sure you can back your hook up. For me, I have a coaching/masterminding group I facilitate. It's my "One-time Your Business" 8 Week Burn. If you don't have a powerful and meaningful hook, take all the time needed to develop one. It's important to do this before you start building your partnerships. Why waste time if you can't truly connect and show your uniqueness. Do it right the first time.

If you are introducing yourself in front of a group and have more time, that is when a 30 second commercial would be appropriate. The only steps you would add...

Who is your ideal client?

What do you want to get out of the event? Have your cards ready to share. I am surprised how many times I'm at an networking event and people do not even come prepared with their business cards. It's crazy. This is just a basic practice.

Represent yourself as a professional. You want to come dressed for success. Your first impression could be your lasting impression. You have one shot to get it right. This too surprises me, some people show up dressed for a very casual occasion, not dressed for a professional event and ready to network.

What about your attitude? If you are in a bad mood or having a bad day then you will take that attitude with you to the networking event. It's better if you don't show up at all. Do you want people to associate this mood with you?

Be a good listener. The key to connecting is to use the 80/20 rule. Listen 80% of the time and share your thoughts 20% of the time. Use the FORD technique: Family, Occupation, Recreation, and Dream. Keep your conversations around these four.

Why do people always ask, "What do you do for a living?" Instead ask a meaningful question, "What do you live to do?"

The three most important things to remember about connecting are: Listen, Listen, and Listen.

It is easy to know how to connect if you just put yourself in the other person's place. How you connect is how others connect as well. If you truly want to connect with someone, ask yourself is the conversation about you or about them? Remember the last time you had a conversation where someone made it all about them? Then remember back to a conversation when the other person let the conversation be about you. Ask yourself what the purpose is of the conversation you are having? Are you trying to connect with them?

Make it about them not about you!

Remember to follow up. The follow up is an important part of the process and many people will drop the ball here. The follow up needs to be prompt and specific. You want to bring up something specific to the conversation you had with them during the networking event. Once you have had small talk and have rekindled the rapport built at the networking event, don't forget to set the appointment!

Admit to yourself that because life is balanced you will not connect to everyone. Don't try forcing a connection but instead move on to connect with someone else who is like you. Life is too short and time is too limited.

Get involved! Join and participate on a board where the other members are people from your target list. You have to be careful not to say yes to more than one or maybe two in any given time because this is a commitment of time and there is only so much time in the day. This is a trap that some professionals will get into and it will distract them from what they need to be doing to keep their business running. If you don't have time to fully commit and do a great job you are better off not taking the role at all. You don't want to fail here!

Know when to say "no."

Another important part of the process is to not lose momentum when participating as a board member. You have spent a lot of time connecting at a high level after the honor of being asked to serve on the board. After your term, make sure you do not stop attending the networking meetings. I see this happen often. You have just gotten started. Why quit now? This makes no sense to me.

Remember it's about quality, not quantity.

I have found that it's easier to manage a smaller number of relationships because I can give quality attention and really make the time for these relationships. Having a large quantity of people to mail, send monthly newsletters, have on an email campaign and include in your social media platforms is good and does not have to have a limit; but when it comes to connecting on a deeper level and building strong business supporters, I feel that twenty relationships is a good target number. If you have made true connections with them, this is all you need to have a very profitable and successful business. Best of all you will have time for all of them.

These are the people you know everything about, you call on a regular basis, remember them on their important days (birthdays, anniversary, etc.), and interact with face to face often. These are people who have the same interests as you and become your lifelong friends. Remember the 80/20 rule. Spend 80% of your time, energy and resources on your core relationships and 20% on the others.

Another good way to meet new professionals that can support your business is to ask for introductions. You have people in your sphere and current partnerships that you can reach out to. Ask for an introduction to the people you want to connect with. When asking for their help, also don't forget to get permission to use their name. With a warm call you will have a much higher chance of landing the appointment.

I like to send an email and cc the person that introduced me then follow up with the phone call.

Why do people always chase after new business when they already have everyone they need. Stop chasing and starting connecting.

How to connect during your follow up meetings – 8 steps

Step 1 - Prepare for the meeting

Tina Mitchell

Do your research before the meeting. This is so easy with social media and the internet. Look on their website and social media platforms to see how they are promoting their business and what is important to them.

A great resource to use is Charlie App. Charlie combs through hundreds of sources and automatically sends you a one-pager on everyone you're going to meet with, before you see them. Pretty amazing tool!

Step 2 - At the meeting start with the most important 2 questions:

"What's working in your business?"
"What needs improvement in your business?"

If you are trying to earn the opportunity to work with them and replace their current partnerships, ask the questions a little differently.

"What is working with your current partnership?"
"What needs improvement with your current partnership?"

What you don't want to do is start with a presentation going over everything you can do for them. They will not hear what you are saying when you are making the meeting about you instead of them. In this type of meeting you want to remember the 80/20 rule once again and let them talk 80% of the time and you talk 20% of the time, just the same as you would at a networking event.

There will be plenty of time for equal conversation after the connection has been made. Once you have built a friendship you will converse as friends do. This is what connection is all about.

Step 3 – Tailor your conversation around these answers

Once you find out the answers to these two important questions this is what you will want to have a conversation around.

You can present what I like to call your "Meetup one-sheet." This is a sheet that bullet points everything you offer in your business. Your service levels, products, processes and unique offerings. Don't leave anything off your "Meetup one-sheet" as they may read it after the meeting and you want all the highlights of your business. BUT, only make reference to the answers to the two questions. If you notice these are not on your "Meetup one-sheet," add them for the next meeting. Just as we discussed in "one-time" your business you want to "one-time" your "Meetup one-sheet."

Step 4 – Ask the next question

"What is important to you now in your life and business?"

This is your opportunity to connect on an emotional level and to learn more about them and what's important to them.

You will know if you are having a successful meeting if they share a lot. This means you have built a connection and they are enjoying the time together.

Step 5 - Ask for the business

"What can I do to earn your business?"

Get a commitment!

Step 6 – Reason to follow up or call to action

Provide a reason to follow up. The ability to follow up is the key to building on the connection you have started.

Step 7 – Stay Connected; Follow up and continue to follow up

Finish what you started and don't lose momentum. Follow up, follow through and be consistent. This is what it takes to build a lasting partnership.

Have you ever left a meeting with someone and afterwards you felt you built a great connection, only to never talk with that person again? This is most likely because you missed this step.

Step away from your computer and connect voice to voice and face to face. Make phone calls on a regular basis and start meeting in person. Inviting someone to lunch or events that don't have anything to do with business can be one of the best ways to connect on a deeper level.

When I make follow up calls I rotate with…

Value, Education, Opportunity, Personal and Fun

> ▸ Call to provide something of **value**. Do you want a response when you call? Ask the right questions.
> "What challenge are you having today that I can solve?"
> "What can I help you with today?"
> "What would make your business better today that I can provide?"
> "What gap in your business do you have today that I can fill?"
> Using the word "today" makes you a possible solution now!

- Call to provide **education** or invite them to an educational event.

  What is happening in the market you can provide education on to help them to be more successful? Find a gap in their business and help fill it.

  Improve their business and they will want to support yours.

- Provide an **opportunity** – What opportunity can you provide that will grow their business? I have many and to list a few... my coaching programs, workshops and my radio show. I will share in more detail below about these. This is powerful, so get creative and help them get more business.

- Call for a **personal** reason – ask how their weekend was, acknowledge a special day or comment on something personal and important to them.

  Do they love sports? Better yet, are they from another state and love a different team? If they do, get that team's schedule and congratulate them when they win.

  Do they have a dog, hobby or something else important to them?

  Provide something fun around something special to them.

  Do you see how this could make them feel good? Make someone feel good and they will want to reciprocate.

Tina Mitchell

- Call to invite them to a **fun** event that has nothing to do with business.

I will share later some of my fun event ideas.

Step 8 – Monitor the partnership

Determine if they will be one of your core partners and receive your higher level of communication that I talked about earlier, or remain as part of your database with minimum and a lower level of communication.

Think out of the box…

When I started as a lounge manager at the Holiday Inn I had to figure out what clientele I wanted to cater to, where they were and go get them.

Who would come into my lounge in the middle of the afternoon? People who went into other lounges during the afternoon! It turned out that in Bellevue, they were retired men. I just had to visit my competitors to figure this out and then strategize on how I would get them over to my establishment.

By the way, one of those establishments soon went out of business.

Another way to connect with the people you want to work with is to provide a platform that will benefit them and their business.

Here are a few things I did in my mortgage business…

- Host a Radio Show

Hosting a weekly radio show provided a space to showcase my current partners and professionals I wanted to build a partnership with.

It made it easy to pick up the phone and get a meeting with almost anyone because I was inviting them to be interviewed on my show.

This also established me as an expert to my clients and referral partners.

- Conduct Workshops

I share my personal and professional core practices through workshops. This was a great way to be a leader in my industry and to share my uniqueness. I tailor my workshop examples to be specific to their business and teach how it will help them succeed.

I recently just launched my *One-time Your Business 8 Week Burn* masterminding and coaching program for real estate professionals and what a hit it is! I am not only helping my partners but also am sharing a philosophy of mine and shining as a unique individual.

- Host Workshops

I host and invite other industry leaders who are in different professions than I am. I discovered speakers that my target audience want to hear and I put the workshop together.

- Fun Events

I plan and host many fun events. It's always good to have an event that has nothing to do with business. This is where I have the opportunity to connect on a friend level and this is my ultimate goal.

You have heard of cookie bakes haven't you? What about hosting a craft make? Just like the white elephant exchange at Christmas, you pick numbers to see who gets whose craft.

What about a cooking class? These are a blast!

Wine and painting anyone? In the Seattle area we have a lot of art studios that offer paining classes and wine.

You can have so much fun with a movie night. Reserve the entire theatre for your group.

For the girls, a massage day.

For the men, a day together at the barber for a shave and cut? Okay, I'm not getting a shave but I am putting the event together.

I have so many other event ideas. If you want more, please reach out to me.

People do business with people they care about and have fun with.

How do you want your business colleagues, your clients and business partners to describe you?

Connecting with others is important.

Remember that making true connections is the key to your success, not just in your professional life, but also your personal life.

Follow Up, Follow Up and Follow Up!

The most important form of follow up, next to face to face, is to pick up the phone. I love that today everything is all about using technology to communicate because a phone call allows me to stand out from the crowd.

To ensure you make phone calls and are consistent with them, you will want to have a Power Hour scheduled every day as I talked about when time blocking. It should be the same time of day, every day. If not scheduled on your calendar, you will most likely not do it. This time should be as important as a client or partner meeting. Would you ever cancel one of these meetings? If the answer is "no," you would not cancel your Power Hour. Power Hour is not about the power of numbers but instead about the power of how many real connections you make.

Focus on value not price, on emotions, not reasons, on benefits, not specifications and talk about them, not about you.

Sending emails? The best thing to put in the subject line is in the form of a question.

Mail? What about "gift shockers?" The name should say it all. You mail a gift that when they open, it is a little shocking (in a good way.) You can have a lot of fun with these.

Here's a few ideas…

Boomerangs - "With me, your clients will keep coming back for more."
Measuring cups – filled with goodies "Success beyond measure."
Pop rocks – "My service will rock your world."
Dice – "Why roll the dice with other lenders – meet with me!"

Tina Mitchell

These are just a few, I have over 50 to help bring a little shock to your target list. Please reach out to me if you want my other ideas.

Handwritten cards! The power of words! In any communication count how many times you use the word "I." Anytime possible replace it with "You." When writing handwritten cards, you should always include a P.S. Another tip, don't use your company stock cards but instead order your own stationary with your branding on it. It's worth the small additional cost.

Social Media? First and foremost, you want to use it! Share things that are happening in your personal and professional life. Have your target list and rotate on a weekly basis to comment on their posts. You will be pleasantly surprised when you see how you can build a connection with adding social media to your reach out's. I hear people say all the time that social media doesn't work for them. That's because they are using it incorrectly. Trust me, it does work!

Rotate your communication reach out efforts with... Phone calls, emails, gift shockers, hand written cards, social media and most importantly, get face to face with them. You now have all the bases covered to truly connect with them.

As I have stated in all my other core practices... Give it time! You will most likely not see results if you don't give it time and stop too soon.

To connect with love ones, colleagues, clients and business partners is to get to know them and they will want to know you. Show them what you can do for them and they will want to know what they can do for you. What people will remember is who you are and how you make them feel. Connect with others and they will want to connect with you!

When you spend quality time with people you produce quality results and relationships.

Get connected and watch your professional and personal relationships explode!

WRAPPING IT ALL UP...

Next Steps To Take Your Life & Business to the Highest Level
(Based on my 6 personal & professional core practices)

Dream

Start visualizing – Examples listed on page 18.

Discover your why exercise – Questions to answer on page 34.

Write your affirmations – My affirmations are on page 43.

Make your plan – Steps to take on page 47.

Be Alert

Make a list of things that make you feel good – See mine on page 51.

Plan your morning (motivation) and evening (inspiration) routines – My routine is on page 65.

Do the Reflection Challenge – See page 79.

Learn to Fail

Do the life is balanced exercise - Shown on page 118.

"One-time Your Business"

"One-timing" exercise – page 140.

Schedule on-time – page 144.

Implement one-timing ideas – Listed on page 165.

Embrace Your Strengths

Do the strengths and weakness test – page 178.

Get Connected

Make a list of your core partners – View page 198.

Write your 10 second commercial – View page 199.

8 Steps to Connect at Follow Up Meeting – View page 204.

Develop your "Meetup one-sheet" – View page 206.

Create your follow ups and reach outs. How often and who will you call, send emails, mail for your "gift shockers," post on social media, write on your handwritten cards, events will you have and who will you get together with. Get insight on page 207.

My book was about my personal and professional core practices. You may have noticed after reading my book that they all intertwine with each other. I can't be successful in any of my core practices without the others. Everything I do in my personal and professional life is based on these six core practices.

The reason I decided to open up and share my personal story is because like you, I have a unique story. I didn't know any other way to share what is important to me without sharing it all, the good and the bad. Without my personal story, I could not truly explain how my core practices were created. The why behind them was important for me to share with you and my life experiences explained how I got to my core practices.

Dream and you will accomplish anything you desire for your life. *Be Alert* and happiness is guaranteed. *Learn to Fail* and success is yours. *One-time Your Business* and take control of your business and your life. *Embrace Your Strengths* and love what you do. *Get Connected* and you will attract all the people you need in your business and life.

These are my personal and professional core practices that direct everything I do in my life. I sincerely hope I was able to provide some inspiration to help you achieve the best personal and professional life. Thank you for taking time out of your busy life to allow me to share my purpose in life: To inspire others to *Live Their Dream*. Remember, you can do it!

Tina Mitchell

If you would like to schedule my *Live Your Dream Now* (personal core practices) workshop or my *Thrive In Your Business* (professional core practices) workshop, please email a request to tinamitchellteam.com.

Live Your Dream Now!
- Tina Mitchell

Tina Mitchell

Tina's Early Childhood

FEDERAL WAY NEWS April 1977
Their best - and more

Lotsa cookies sold

GIRL SCOUTS from the Totem Council, South Sound Association, Potlatch and Lakota Service areas who sold more than 100 boxes of Girl Scout cookies in the recent drive gathered this week. In the front, Tina Frisbey, a seven-year-old from Troop 1205, sold 400 boxes. Next to her kneeling is Jeana Giangrasso of Troop 15 who sold 200 boxes. In the back row, from left, are Tina Isreal, Laura Krussel, Vicky Joslin, Betsy David, Karen Peterson, Jessica Champie, Teresia Sundstrom, Michelle Werner, Kim Pigg, Jamie Erhardt and Diane Acheson. Not picutred are Gretchen Hewlett who sold 200 boxes and Suzanne Niedermeyer who sold 133 boxes.

REHEARSING FOR their part in the May 9 spring concert of the Thalia Youth Symphonies are Karen, left, and Tina Frisbey, daughters of Mr. and Mrs. Gerd Frisbey of Federal Way. Five-year-old Karen is the youngest member of Thalia. She plays in both the Beginning Strings and in the Symphonette orchestra. Tina is in the Cadet Symphony.

Local girls to appear in youth symphony concert

Karen and Tina Frisbey, daughters of Mr. and Mrs. Gerald Frisbey of 3641 SW 330th St., in Federal Way, will be among the young musicians who will perform when the Thalia Youth Symphonies present their spring concert Sunday, May 9, at the Seattle Center Playhouse.

Karen, who is five years old, plays in the Beginning Strings and in the Symphonette Orchestra. This will be her first appearance in concert. Sister Tina is in the Cadet Symphony. Both are violinists.

The preparatory orchestras will perform at 1 p.m., starting with the Beginning Strings. These very young Thalia musicians, under the guidance of Lillian Claunch, will play Gretchaninoff's "Out For a Walk." They will be followed by the Symphonettes, the youngest of the three orchestras. David Harris, senior associate conductor, directs this orchestra.

The Cadet Symphony, an intermediate orchestra, will next perform three selections, including "Trumpet Voluntary" by Purcell. Keith Eisenrey, a Bellevue student,

will conduct this number. He is a junior associate conductor and percussionist for Thalia Youth Symphony.

At 4 p.m., the Youth Symphony concert will feature two gifted young piano soloists, Karen Janes and Kazumi Bando, both winners of the 1975 Thalia concerto auditions. Besides piano, Karen plays the double string bass in both the Thalia and Seattle youth symphonies. She will perform Gershin's Rhapsody in Blue Thirteen-year-old Kazumi Bando, a temporary resident of Seattle from Japan, appeared with the Seattle Sym-

phony last May as a concerto winner of the 1975 Seattle Young Artists Festival. She will perform Mozart's Piano Concerto.

During the intermission, four women and four men of the Puget Sound area will be presented with Civic Achievement awards for outstanding communication in the arts.

The Thalia Youth Symphonies are co-directed by Frances Walton and Michael Scheramerstew

Tickets will be available at the Playhouse the day of the concert or may be obtained in advance by calling Molly Petro at 746-0293.

Tina and Karen perform with the Thalia Youth Symphony.

Music contest winners
1977 slate Money Tree date

The young winners of the recent Pierce-King County Musical Festival will stage an hour program at the Moneytree Restaurant in Federal Way Friday, June 3 at 8 p.m.

A group of Irish and Scottish dancers who are also champions will appear on the same program. Singer Miguel Anaya and Fred Pieske, two times international accordian champion, will also perform.

Rita Kucklack who has a studio in Federal Way and also teaches at Highline Community College, is in charge of the program.

Admission to the program is free.

The young performers include Pana Nelson, Jay Ball, Pam Siegler, Kim Clark, Duane Kochel, Karen Frisbie, Donald Helmholz, Tina Frisbie, Jeff Poskin and Eric Saasbad.

More Performing, Awards and Practice

Tina's Pre-teen Years

The News Sunday, May 28, 1978

Trophy winners

LOCAL MUSICIANS, five top winners from the recent King Pierce County Music Competition were honored at a recital held at the Money Tree last week. They were, back row, left to right, Mark Theadore, accordion; David Holmquist, classic guitar; Caroline Boden, flute. Front row, Tina Frisbey, violin and Kim Sojak, folk guitar who also received a $50 scholarship.

TINA MITCHELL

Career achievements in Tina's earliest years in her mortgage profession.

Mortgage Originator

Top 200 Originators

Niche Marketing

2001
Top 200 - Number of Loans

Tina Mitchell

AFTERWORD & ACKNOWLEDGMENTS

Please read the thoughts below to know who Tina is from the voice of others. Each of these people is an important part of the journey that I have shared with you and that is the reason I wanted them included.

Beth Samuelson - Tina's Mom

"I am incredibly proud of the person Tina has become. As a child she was wise beyond her years. Even then she was capable of channeling her determination toward positive and intelligent outcomes. She was able to focus on the means to achieve a positive result."

We would get to take the train. The girls would perform their violins for women's meetings. On those trips, the girls would practice in the women's lounge. People would make comments and ask them to perform in other cars. One time a man said, 'These children deserve a fine meal' and we were able to eat in the dining car. Whenever we'd take the Amtrak Coast Starline, Tina would play her violin on the train. She had to spend 2-3 hours a day practicing to stay in the symphony as a 5 year old. It's how she became who she is."

"Tina learned early that you didn't get things for nothing. She was always a hard worker. In junior high after our family dynamic got too hard for her to handle, Tina got in trouble at school and had to go to school on Saturdays as part of the punishment. I got a call from the school and was told that Tina worked harder than all of the kids put together. In one day she had worked enough to make up for the rest of the year. They wanted to hold her up as an example to the other kids."

"I used to take Tina and her sister to the train station when things got bad at home. If you can let go, when you go back, problems are not so monumental. We'd sit there and talk about where we'd want to go. We'd talk about future trips."

Karen Kelly - Tina's Little Sister

"Daily I am amazed at the woman Tina is, because I know where she came from. Tina is resilient and generous. Everything she has, she fought for, so you'd think she'd want to hang on to it, but she would give it all. She's very well-rounded. I wonder, 'how many times can she get knocked down and just get back up?' She's just adaptable and steadfast and so genuine. What you see is what you get in home or business... who she is inside never changes. There is no mask that Tina wears."

"Tina has always been bigger than life. She would do whatever it took to get whatever she wanted, but she had a sense of integrity. Tina understood that life was not fair and always had a sense that you have to reach for and grab it and feel good about it in the end."

"Both of us created who we could become as adults - back then we didn't realize, but the train station gave us an opportunity to dream. We talked about where people went. I would pretend I was in certain families. Tina would imagine who she would become."

"Tina always gave 100% in whatever she did. She was always able to dream big and imagine big."

Dave Mitchell - Tina's Husband

"Tina and I have been married for 20 years and I would describe her as loving, trustworthy, hardworking, giving, upbeat, positive and all around a nice person. Most importantly she is beautiful inside and out. Through the years we have become closer than I could have ever imagined. She has definitely made me a more patient person."

"What I have observed over the years that makes Tina different from other people is she has the ability to completely shut off work and relax. If you observe Tina and see all she has on her plate you may think this would not be possible but she has proven it is. She has always blended into any circumstance and has a good time,

Tina Mitchell

always making the most out of any situation good or bad. It's been amazing to watch the way she works and continues to work towards her dreams without giving up! When she told me she was writing a book I said, "You have to be kidding" but I knew she would do it. I have observed her working for hours with no sleep and completely embracing the experience."

"I know people will benefit from her professional and personal core practices if they embrace them. They will have more free time to do the things they truly enjoy doing in life. Her book is insightful!"

"I am very proud of my wife!"

Stephanie Mitchell - Tina's Stepdaughter

"Tina has such a unique story. She went from being a waitress at Denny's with no college or formal training to having her own company and being in the top 1 % of her industry? Her story of "How do you get from point a to b?" was what she shared at the House of Hope. I went with her and it was an amazing experience. Before we went, we talked about how all these women have nothing and it would be good for them to see that they can do anything.

House of Hope is a program where women have a chance to rebuild their lives over a twelve month period, allowing for real change. When Tina shared her story, there were lots of tears - the women were really touched. It was great to meet and hear their stories and connect on that level. They asked her to come back.

Tina is different. She has a very big heart, like a big ball of love. She is one of the sweetest people and has the biggest heart. She's like a little kid, she gets excited easily. I think her book will touch a lot of people, like a Lifetime movie.

When I was a kid, she worked so much, for Tina there is no work life balance. When I came out for summers, she always made time for me though. She probably never slept. We'd stay up to 2 a.m. and then a few hours later, she'd be off to work.

I love her and her spirit and energy. Tina is always very positive and great to be around.

Stephanie McCarthy - Tina's Best Friend and Owner/Realtor of Real Living Northwest Realtors

"Seven years ago, the force of Tina Mitchell entered my life and our spiritual, dreamer and business playground opened up. I have not met a person who is more dedicated to her processes, that not only allow her to stand above the rest in her mortgage profession, but also are dearly embraced on her personal growth side. Tina is so incredibly organized and I am wowed with her enthusiasm for her profession and with life. She is uber-passionate about how she does it and - all that positive energy - oozes onto you."

"We had a similar vision and started creating vision boards together. We were both on a spiritual journey and created a vision board retreat for others in our profession, to allow us to grow personally and professionally."

"At my office, we refer to Tina as the anomaly; you give her an idea and it sparks something in her to put a process together. She just drives with any passion she has and it all comes together so beautifully."

"We all have these big dreams and things that we want to do, but we get bogged down. Tina has a dream and she fulfills that dream. I can't respect her enough. She's so incredibly powerful. She has built her character and turned all her life experiences into a positive. You can't help but be positive when you are around Tina."

Tina Mitchell

"She lives through her core practices and beliefs and is one of the most real people that I've met. Aside from being my best friend, she is such a mentor to me in so many ways."

"This book has so many levels. It's geared for business professionals, but the tools she shares work for personal experience, too. Tina helps you to create a balance so you can have more time for your family and doing what you're passionate about. She's always about putting a process together."

"A lot of people in our industry look at Tina and see and admire her processes and coaching mechanisms; they never see more until she starts sharing her personal story. There's so much incredible depth to Tina and her depth is what makes her so amazing. Her book will help people see how amazing she truly is! Move over Oprah and Tony Robbins, Tina's coming through! "

Debra Trappen - Tina's Friend and Founder and CEO D11 Consulting

"Tina really wants the best for everyone including herself. In a group, she's not her effervescent self - she is very reserved - she's an assessor and analyzer to the core of who she is."

"When Tina speaks it's very business oriented. She doesn't open up to that personal side of things and she doesn't really open the kimono. This book will help people by showing them Tina's personal process and progress - as a mortgage professional and individual. It will inspire them to be better and reach for more, like the caterpillar to the butterfly. The right people will finally be able to find her [with this book] because she is really telling her story."

"Anybody who owns a small business will benefit from the book and her philosophy of "working on" vs. "working in" and streamlining processes and system. Almost every time we talk we find something we can "One-time." I don't actually see it right away, but it's there!"

"It's a cool philosophy. 'One-timing' could easily become like Google-ing." Tina's prime audiences are real estate, mortgage, individual insurance agents - anyone who is kind of on their own, but not really on your own."

"Tina is tenacious, relentless, and focused... when you start peeling the onion, you discover she is so beautiful. The opportunity to truly know her is a blessing and I'm really excited that this book allows more people to get to do this. What I love... is that I can hear her reading this to me. Her message has never been clearer, more confident and strong."

Dan Wingard, Tina's Friend, Realtor for Keller Williams and Life Coach -

"Tina is definitely not a diva. She handles herself with the utmost professionalism. She has compassion, attention, and under stress, that is pretty amazing. It was so rewarding for me to see her come alive [through the making of 'Dream']. She practically jumped out of her skin - overflowing with joy."

"She's headed for big things at whatever level she wants to take it. It's fun to connect with people who are clear about their intention and to see their growth and the growth of our relationship, being that to the core. I think lots of people will be impacted by her book, in the field that she's in - mortgage, as well as real estate, entrepreneurs, and anyone that just wants to make an impact on this world in a positive way. Also, people who are going through changes - hers is a story of challenge, overcoming, and embracing the present. It's a story of the ages that is good for everyone."

"Tina has a heart to serve and wants to create a space for people to live their dreams. She comes from such an authentic place - a heart to serve - not from the mindset of 'I could be successful if...'"

Cathy Waidelich - Tina's Friend, CEO and Founder Legacy Caring

"I've seen Tina present her "One-time Your Business" and "Live Your Dream Now" workshops and she is an incredibly effective presenter. Tina shares how her tools free up our time to focus on our dreams; she captured my mind, body and soul. She is professional, composed and an amazing role model. Her authentic story-telling and method of sharing ways to free up time to focus on our passion captures our heartstrings.

Tina is multi-talented! She launched the song she wrote, "Dream" during a LegacyCaring event, and it has become our theme song. It's inspiring, just like Tina, who has overcome so many challenges throughout her life.

She's one of those beautiful people who've been through a lot."

"Tina can see where people are, where they want to be and offer them a roadmap to get there."

"Tina has a beautiful heart, is giving and caring. I imagine this book will launch her into a whole new phase of her career and life. I can see her sharing it on Oprah's SuperSoul Sunday - it's such a meaningful story that needs to be shared with the world."

Jerry North - Tina's General Manager at the Federal Way Denny's

"When I first met Tina, she was 19 years old. She was pretty naive and I remember it being so ironic. She told me her story - her husband was in state prison and she needed to support herself. He had tried to rob a Winchell's Donut Shop. It made me laugh, because Denny's owned the donut chain, so it was funny that she would share that story. She was very smiley and energetic, and nervous but willing to work graveyard. She had no experience but there was a quality about her so I gave her a chance. Tina has always been driven by customer satisfaction and making

money. She had the looks, drive and commitment to make customers happy which would make her money. I have a ton of respect for her commitment and her drive. I asked her once, 'When is it going to be enough?' and she looked at me like I had three eyes. Tina always wants to do more and just keeps going. She's the perfect example of commitment and focus to get things done."

Roger Savy - Tina's Mentor and Friend

"Tina is authentic, naive, and a fabulous scholar. She has so much to share. Tina is desperate to improve the world and has such a sense of contribution. She feels the pain of the world and feels she can change it. It just pours out of her. She never gives up. She is almost a little delusional in that she believes she can change the destiny of the future. Once she has focused on an objective, be it a person, project, town or community, her tenacity reigns supreme.

She shows that success is simple, but not easy. I think this book is a chance for her to share the lessons she's captured, to record them and share."

Iral Nelson - Tina's Friend and Builder of the Excel Spreadsheet That Advanced Into Her Software Mortgage Triangle Software

"Tina always wanted to make sure her clients understood the process and their choices. She was clearly an educator! She was a very hard worker, diligent, and determined. She is more focused on developing processes and tools than most people. They just accept the tools they are handed, and do their jobs. Not Tina. When I first met her, she'd only been in the mortgage industry for a few years, but she was already determined to create better tools and processes than anything she had used or seen."

"Tina and I worked on the Excel project regularly for many years until she started developing her software and the MTS project began. It was the longest project I've ever worked on (except for supporting Tina in general – I still help her with things occasionally). Working on the Excel project required a lot of time and focus. There were hundreds of complex formulas to design, keep track of, and modify. Sometimes

Tina Mitchell

Tina would realize that a major change was needed on some component of the spreadsheet system — her original design for that part wasn't actually getting her what she needed, so we'd fix it, or even scrap it, and start the component over."

"We spent many long hours into the late evenings on the project. Sometimes we'd get so tired; we'd start getting a little bit frustrated, but kept at it! We spent so much time on that project (and others), that we got to know each other really well over the years."

"Clearly, she can dream, and she knows what to do with what she sees. When she sets a goal, she'll do whatever it takes, however long it takes, to achieve it. She's thoughtful and purposeful about everything she does, both professionally and personally. She's helped more people than I can count over the years, created more relationships (both professional and personal), and has had a great impact on me as well. (Tina was my first client, and a number of others were later introduced to me by her.)

I continue to find new insights that can apply to me just as much as anyone else. She is loyal, caring, and trustworthy. She's a confident dreamer and doer. I should also add that she's resourceful, determined, and talented. Come to think of it, when she has time, she's pretty fun too! She has a lot to share, and it's important to her to do that."

Todd Elston - Tina's Friend and Managing Partner Mortgage Triangle Software

"When you first start working with someone, you don't know to what degree they are willing to give up their integrity in order get what they want. I have known Tina for 7 years. Over time, I have learned to trust her business instincts. Having created 3 successful startups before, I have my preferred ways of doing things, especially related to technology."

"So overtime, she has taken on more ownership in terms of the what we are trying to accomplish as a business even to the point of managing technical resources. That is not saying she doesn't get stuck, but what I like is when she goes down a rabbit hole in term of technical approach, she is not afraid to ask for help and is very professional even when I get frustrated."

"I have worked with quite a few partners over the years, I would rather have someone take ownership and make decisions and move forward, rather than be indecisive and let a problem languish."

"Tina is not a victim. She takes ownership of what she believes in and follows through without blaming others for approaches that may or may not work out. She takes ownership, but it can be a two edged sword. It is possible to have help where dreams are concerned and with the proper team synergy, a person can leap forward in almost a non-linear fashion to realize a goal. You don't have to be a hero in order to realize your dream."

"Tina always moves forward and is very successful in realizing a goal. There are people that love her and are willing to help to the degree of whatever it takes to get her there."

"I appreciate intelligence regardless of how people utilize it to get to where they are or where they are going. I also evaluate what would happen if we make a lot of money, since people get weird where money is concerned. Tina, seemed to have a strong definition of who she is and what her goals are. I also look at the business case and the partner's ability to follow through. I don't have any concerns about my ability to deliver on the business and technical side, but I do have concerns about a partner's ability to market and sell a product, especially where a new brand is concerned. Basically I liked what I heard. There are times when you buy something and no matter what the cost is you feel good about it even if the item purchased fails, and that is how I felt about Tina."

"Trust her instincts even if you disagree. Her approach is different than mine. I like to approach things through known and existing paths. Ways that I know will work, since I have successfully done it that way before. Tina is willing to jump right in and trust that everything will work out. I don't like surprises, I guess, and Tina is a bit of a surprise. She is an "edifice of intent." Basically, she creates her own goals and structures them in a way that makes them so palpable so that others can work within the same context."

Ron Poborsky - Tina's Friend and Manager at Wells Fargo, Currently a Sales Manager for Caliber Home Loans

"Tina was introduced to me as super go-getter. When she came on to Wells Fargo she was kinda green and needed direction but she was so driven and anal about all the details. It was not uncommon for her to pull an all-nighter. I would say, 'Are you insane? Go to bed.'"

"Sometimes you need to try to motivate people to work harder - that was never Tina's deal. She's all in - after extra credit. Always asking... what can I do to make it more comprehensive? She had the drive to create the best mortgage presentation. There are very few people that have the drive to hang with something as long as she has. I used to ask her 'why reinvent the wheel' and her response was always 'why wouldn't you?'"

"The first time homebuyer seminars were the big break. Tina came in to make it happen! She went all-in, 4 a weekend for 3-4 years, she hit it really hard. Then she started new construction and killed it in that project, too. You couldn't outwork Tina."

"She was a classical violinist and didn't pursue it - never would do it - I was never sure why. I know she had not a great childhood and a husband with issues and I think she was determined, 'I'm going to show people I can be a success.'"

"Sometimes you meet people that say I'll be happy when... She was so driven to reach milestones. She would sacrifice everything to be successful in business. More than just work. She can't imagine not working so hard on certain things. As you looked at how hard Tina worked, you just shook your head."

"I'm thrilled to see her write a book. I'm sure she'll take it on the road and sell this thing - it'll probably be a lifetime movie - seminars were just a stepping stone."

Jen Miller - Tina's Friend and Book Editor Who Helped Make "Journey With Me" Happen

"Tina's story quantifies determination and perseverance and is truly an amazing read. Interviews with Tina's friends, family, coworkers, and mentors and discussions with Tina herself showed me an amazingly gifted and giving woman. Her attention to detail and following best practices is commendable. I am grateful to have been a part of sharing Tina's story."

Words alone cannot thank each of you enough for being a part of my life and my journey. Thank you for contributing to my book and to the person I am today.

- Tina

ABOUT THE AUTHOR

Tina is with Absolute Mortgage and has been in the mortgage industry for 20 years. She has been recognized in the top 1% Mortgage Producers Nationwide multiple times throughout her career.

Tina is a radio personality and host of The Money Hour on 1150 AM KKNW.

Tina is committed to the Real Estate community and has been awarded Partner Of The Year from Washington REALTORS, Media Of The Year from Seattle King County REALTORS, and has served on the board for Women's Council of REALTORS.

She is a numbers gal, so much that she designed and hired a developing team to build an advanced mortgage analysis web based software to help educate her clients on their loan options. She is Founder and Owner of Mortgage Triangle Software which is available on the market for mortgage professionals nationwide.

Tina is a natural speaker and shares her personal and professional practices in the form of workshops with the business community and homeless shelters in her local market. She also coaches and mentors other business professionals.

Tina is very excited to have now published her first book on her personal and professional core practices and looks forward to writing again in the future.

Tina Mitchell

SCHEDULE YOUR WORKSHOP

Live Your Dream Now **Workshop**

This workshop is based on Tina's personal core practices; *Dream*, *Be Alert* and *Learn To Fail*. Discover what's important in life and find your why behind your dream. Embrace the beauty that is all around you, and most importantly, to recognize that life is balanced. This is a dynamic workshop with breakout sessions to work on you dream, your purpose and what's important in life. Like Tina has, experience your "aha" moments and you will be changed forever.

Thrive In Your Business **Workshop**

This workshop is based on Tina's professional core practices; *One-time Your Business*, *Embrace Your Strengths* and *Get Connected*. Build a business model that is efficient, consistent and replicable. Learn how to embrace your strengths and hire a team so you can enjoy your professional and personal life. Get connected with the people you need in your business and they will want to help you succeed. By embracing Tina's professional core practices you can truly live a balanced life, make the income you want and love what you do!

Tina Mitchell

SPECIAL THANKS

I would personally like to thank the following:

Jen Miller, my Editor - NeedSomeoneTo.com

Antwane Tyler for the cover photo - AntwaneTylerPhotography.com

Dave Mosso for the book cover design - SpaciousMind.com

Olivia Carriveau for editing photos of me growing up.

Also, I'd like to express gratitude to my family and friends mentioned in my book. Without them, *Journey With Me* would never have come to life.

And lastly, I would like to thank you, my reader for picking up my book and taking time out of your day to be a part of my journey!